ON THE LIFE OF
LINDA J ALBERTANO
FROM TRAUMA TO HIGH ART

ON THE LIFE OF
LINDA J. ALBERTANO
FROM TRAUMA TO HIGH ART

WITH
FRANK LUTZ

FOREWORD BY
SUZANNE LUMMIS

QUIET TIME PUBLISHING
Hollywood, California 90028

On the Life of Linda J. Albertano with Frank Lutz

ISBN: 978-1-884743-10-8

© 2024 by Linda J. Albertano and Frank Lutz
All Rights Reserved.

To reproduce or utilize this work, permission from the publisher, distributor or copyright owner is required, except for use in a review. Please write editor@quiettimepublishing.com

Library of Congress Control Number: 2024905806

Library of Congress Cataloging-in-Publication Data:
Authors: Linda J. Albertano and Frank Lutz
Title: On the Life of Linda J. Albertano
Foreword: Suzanne Lummis
Identifiers: LCCN
ISBN: 978-1-884743-30-6 (Hardback)
ISBN: 978-1-884743-10-8 (Paperback)
ISBN: 978-1-884743-11-5 (E-book)
Subjects: Women's Rights, Poetry, Performance Art, Music, Film

Cover image by Aldo Mauro

Book design by Kat Georges
KG Design International

Quiet Time Publishing
Deborah Granger, Alex Carmona
www.quiettimepublishing.com

For more information about
Linda J. Albertano, please visit
www.lindajalbertano.com

IN LOVING MEMORY OF
LINDA J. ALBERTANO

My wife and the Love of my Life,
a great artist, and
the finest person I have ever known.
—*Frank Lutz*

TABLE OF CONTENTS

Acknowledgments i
Apologia iii

PART I
Critical Acclaim for Linda J. Albertano 2
Foreword by Suzanne Lummis 6

PART II
L'Amour Pour Toujours 10
The Optimist 13
The Love Ache 15
On the Life of Linda J. Albertano 19
Epilogue 27
Postscript 29

PART III
Welcome to the Life of Linda J. Albertano 32

PART IV
Why I Became a Writer *by Linda J. Albertano* 92
The Way We Were: Nearly Fatal *by Suzanne Lummis* 95

Poems & Stories by Linda J. Albertano
Favorite Memories of Beyond Baroque 99
To the Pacific 102
Beloved 107
All Night Long 108
Après La Pandémie 111
The Real Housewives of the River Styx 112
Busy 113
God's Favorite Angel 116
Black Duck Down 121
Mr. Teenage California 122

Buck Fush 123
Good Americans 125
Mercenary Children 127
Underpopulation 129
She Liked Her Coffee 131
SOS 132
The Skin of the Western World 134
Tokyo Rose 138
Valentine's Day with Lucifer 140
Virtue 145
Lunatic Fringe 149
On Becoming an American Bolonist 151
Frank's Dad 156
Linda's Interview with Gerry Fialka 159

PART V
Frank's Poetry

Warm Italian Night 165
Perugian Souls 166
Renaissance Night 167
A Psalm 168
Moth and Flame 169
Years From Now 170
D Day, Normandy—June 6, 1944 171
Lancasters over Canada 172
Soldier's Night 176
The Cavalier 177
The Hunters 178
My German Ancestor 179
The Funeral 182
The Namesake 191
Zanzibar, 1963 193
UHURU! 195
About Frank Lutz 201

ACKNOWLEDGMENTS

I would like to thank the following people whose kind and loving support helped me deal with Linda's illness from the time we first knew about it in April 2022 to her passing in September 2022 and up to the present day, September 6, 2023. As of this date, it has been one year since our second wedding, held at UCLA Hospital, Santa Monica, CA, in Linda's room. The most joyous day of both of our lives. The saddest day came a week later, on September 13, 2022. Linda and I loved each other very much for well over fifty years. I apologize in advance if I omit anyone, I am grateful to you all.

In particular, I would like to thank certain people who loved Linda over many decades, and were devoted to her memory by helping me with various projects about and for her since she died, and continue to do so: Scott Wardlaw and family, and Alex Carmona, who have spent months sorting through Linda's bodies of work in four artistic disciplines—poetry, performance art, music, and film—in preparing those archives for delivery to the Getty Museum in Los Angeles. These folks also collaborated in making a beautiful film showing Linda in photographs and performance over more than fifty years of her life. Alex also has been instrumental in helping me with the book I have created about Linda's life in art. Also, I would like to thank Charles and Tobi Duncan for helping me sort through Linda's personal effects and beautiful clothing, a very touching experience for all of us.

I would also like to thank our ace bookkeeper, Bob Mitchell, who met Linda fifty years ago, and started a musical trio together, with Bob on the piano, and Linda on guitar and vocals. Also, I would like to thank Quentin Ring, Director of the world-famous poetry venue in Venice, Beyond Baroque, who has been instrumental in helping me craft the Linda J. Albertano Scholarship for Poets. I would like to thank Deborah Granger, a good friend of ours for decades, who has been working diligently with me on editing the Linda book and brings several decades of her expertise in the book and creative arts milieu. Her creativity and discipline are invaluable to me and know no bounds! I want to express my sincere gratitude to Kat Georges and Peter Carlaftes for their creative book design, as well as Ashlyn Petro for the final review before publication.

In addition to the above, the following notable friends have been wonderful in their support of Linda's memory: Anna Homler, Nico & Hanne Mohl, Steve & Melissa Crothers, Joseph Staretski, Ole & Ulla Nielsen, Patricia McDonough, Sabrina Gilliard, Daniela Escamilla, Geri Cvitanovich, Rob Levy, Jean Caby, Des Walsh, Leslie Stanford, Bruce & Fran Peters, Greco Garcia, Nick Olaerts, Erin Blackwell, Bill Messmer, S.A. Griffin, Tom Fries, Taj Mahal, Ann Barton, Prince Diabaté, Suzanne Lummis, Sheila Pinkel, Laurel Ann Bogen, Josie Roth, Elisha Shapiro, Cheryl & Bob Leathers, Gary & Cydney Mandel, Keith & Ginette Koenig, Kennon Raines, Susan Hayden, Suzy Williams, Pegarty Long, Gerry Fialka, Keith Martin, Mauro Monteiro, and David Rosenfeld.

On a final note, I express my gratitude to the friends who endorsed Linda's work and made a significant impact on her life. You will hear more about them in this book.

—Frank Lutz

PUBLISHER'S NOTE:
We also want to acknowledge the following artists for their contributions to this book:

Suzy Williams, singer extraordinaire

Alexis Rhone Fancher, photographer

Mark Savage, photographer

Aline Smith, photographer

Greg Tucker, Nearly Fatal Women photographer

Pegarty Long's Philomenian, Venice Poetry Wall at Venice Beach photographer

APOLOGIA

Dear Reader,
To all the talented photographers who captured breathtaking images of Linda for this book about her life, we, the author, editors, publisher, and technicians involved in its creation, sincerely apologize for not having a record of your names.

Prior to her departure, Linda left a pile of photos, newspaper articles, and reviews of her performances and readings on her desk. Unbeknownst to Frank, she indirectly communicated to him her intention to pursue their shared dream of creating a poetry book. Although she is not here, we present this book on her life with a mix of sorrow and happiness.

PART I

CRITICAL ACCLAIM FOR LINDA J. ALBERTANO

LAUREL ANN BOGEN
Founding Member of Nearly Fatal Women, poet, and author

Linda Albertano, a force of nature, a woman of integrity, a singular voice of unimpeachable honesty. A goddess who rose from childhood trauma and created art that left audiences breathless. She was my friend. Always.

S.A. GRIFFIN
Poet, actor, and Dadaist Supreme

A deeply compassionate and transformative performance artist and poet-writer, Linda J. Albertano was without peer. It is impossible not to be touched by the magic of her boundless humanity and love for all.

QUENTIN RING
Director, Beyond Baroque

Whether you knew Linda from her utterly original performance art, or from her Kora playing, or from hearing her read, or from simply spending time with her in conversation, she was always truly a poet. She breathed life into language, and expanded our sense of what is possible. She has left her poems as a gift to us all, and for that I am truly thankful. They will continue to transform the imaginations of all of us who encounter them.

PRINCE DIABATÉ
Kora Master, Guinea, West Africa (Translated from the French by Frank Lutz)

For my Big Sister Linda J. Albertano, my advisor, my student, she was a Grand Lady, very special in my life. I am composing your song, my sister Linda's song in the Zone of the Spirit and with us. Thank you very much, my Linda, from my heart, and with gratitude. Your Kora instructor since 1999.

ANNA HOMLER
Poet and performance artist

She was an awe-inspiring presence, performance poet and film maker. Linda was a great soul, larger than life and utterly brilliant. She was infinitely kind and utterly brilliant. Life will never be the same without her. Dearest Linda, in your own words, "I will worship at your shrine, forever."

TAJ MAHAL
Great Blues Artist

If there ever was a Creative, Very Feminine, Amazon Goddess of the sweetest nature & temperament that this or any other world has ever seen or known, it has to have been my dear musical friend, the late Linda "Albert" Albertano.
Always smiling and happy, so much so
even her laughter sparkled with musical notes!
Moving with the ancient grace of a gazelle, I never once saw her compromise her glorious height with no man, woman,
child or musician!
Absolutely stunning
woman!
She wrote volumes of poetry, songs, was a wonderful performance artist, played guitar, sang
and so much more!

I was recently able to play one of my all time favorite songs of Linda's, called "2:10 Train"
This concert, which featured The Taj Mahal Quartet and a
very lovely friend from both our pasts named Pamela Poland!
The combination of the quartet, Pamela's strong performance, warm and soothing voice & vocal, mesmerized
the sold out audience!
They responded with thunderous applause!
Thrilled doesn't even come close to how it felt!
We KNOW SHE heard us!!:))
Peace & Beauty
(Rest In Power)

ADAM LEIPZIG
Producer, director, stage, and performance art productions

When we opened the Los Angeles Theatre Center in 1985, performance art had already matured and was moving forward along different and divergent pathways. We had to do a performance art series and we had to get Linda J. Albertano. Linda was flattered to be asked, surprised even, which surprised me, because I had only seen her in performance, and her work struck me as so singular she'd be difficult to convince. "What do you do there?" Linda asked me. "I'm the dramaturg and producing this series," I said. "Of course I'll do it," said Linda. She even knew what a dramaturg was!

Of performance art's divergent pathways at the time, Linda had made the unequivocal decision for performance. She talked, she sang, she moved. She spoke poetry, changed costumes and characters. She had the capacity concentrate herself and expand herself into each situation. When she concentrated herself, her body reduced, became smaller and more vulnerable. This was part of her art, because in life she was taller than most everyone around. When she expanded, you could have sworn she was eight feet tall.

Did I mention the marching band? Yes, there was a marching band. Thirty high schoolers from South LA, dancers, and poets too, all brought together by Linda for her epic piece "Joan of Compton." The band was out in front on Spring Street, drums beating time as they warmed up. Across the street, windows opened at the Alexandria Hotel, a hotel that had once been grand but was now SRO, windows opened, curses hurled, empty 7 Crown bottles hurled too, glass shattered everywhere. We brought the band inside, and Joan of Compton went on. This performance of identity and sacrifice, interrogating the role of women, of suburbs' contrast with central city, of self-realization and self-abnegation being a white person in diverse society.

Where was the truest performance, Linda wondered later, in our 99-seat black box theatre, or in the glass on asphalt outside?

In more recent years we had the privilege of publishing some of Linda's poems in Cultural Daily, and her memories of performing for USO in Vietnam. Whether in words written or spoken, in poetry or prose, in music and in physical presence, her light transcended shape and form. That was her pathway!

PETER CARLAFTES & KAT GEORGES
Poets, publishers and leaders in the Dada art movement

Linda Albertano was a one-of-a-kind artist and human being. Her poetry and performance art was so earth-shatteringly original, it made us all aspire to raise the stakes of our own work. But an artist is more than their art, and Linda was equally defined by her kindness, her humor, and her indefatigable support of other creators. For many years, Linda has been a beloved member of our worldwide Dada family, performing with us in Los Angeles, San Francisco, and New Orleans, with original work, in a staged reading, embodying New York Dada legend Baroness Elsa von Freytag Loringhoven, and more. We miss her daily, and thrive on the memory of our time together.

FOREWORD

BY SUZANNE LUMMIS

After we've noted that Linda J. Albertano thrived in Los Angeles as a force of nature and fount of mischievous intelligence and performative creations; after we've remarked upon the ways she seemed always larger than life, as well as—at 6'4"—taller than most; after we've marveled at her triumphant career in the edgiest art despite being silenced, abused and exploited in Evangelical and Fundamentalist Christian foster homes during much of her youth . . .

We must not omit this. She was funny.

Here is the opening of one of her performance pieces:

> *She Liked Her Coffee, the way she liked her men.*
>
> *Obsequious and fawning.*
>
> *I'm parched!*
>
> *Could you bring me a Dr. Brown's Celery Tonic, please? . . .*

Linda Albertano will be sorely, no madly missed, or—said otherwise in the more effective active tense—we in the literary and arts world of Venice (and regions east of the ocean front, north and south) will miss her.

And now, finally, to the personal first person: I will miss her, her bounteous performances, our trips to the movies—and how she enjoyed nearly all of them, even the crummy ones—our long, phone conversations about politics and other matters, immortal and. It was my good luck to have played a role in her life, and she in mine.

Thanks to Frank Lutz for compiling this record of her indelible contributions to the performance arts monde, and to the common good.

—Suzanne Lummis
Poet and founding member of Nearly Fatal Women 6/13/23

ABOUT SUZANNE LUMMIS

Suzanne Lummis was the fifth recipient of Beyond Baroque Literary Arts Center's George Drury Smith Award for Excellence in Poetry and a 2018/19 City of Los Angeles Fellow, an endowment to artists and writers enabling them to create a new body of work. She is among the few who've defined the poem noir, and poetry.la produces her series on film noir and contemporary poetry, "They Write by Night," featuring poems by poets local and national.

In 2023 she guest-edited a special Noir issue of the international publication Pratik, which features poetry, fiction, non-fiction and essays exploring noir subject matter in the noir style. The *Los Angeles Times* named her poem, "Really Mystic River" one of 14 essential Los Angeles "poems or collections of poetry" in its article "The Ultimate L.A. Bookshelf." She's published three poetry collections, *Idiosyncrasies*, *In Danger*, and Open 24 Hours, the last a winner of the Blue Lynx Prize, and published by Blue Lynx Press, and her poems have appeared in literary publications across the country and in *The New Yorker*. Her phone calls to Linda J. Albertano and Laurel Ann Bogen with the suggestion "Let's join forces and make something happen" led to the founding of Nearly Fatal Women.

PART II

Linda's husband, Frank, wrote these three poems in the final year of her life. He recently appended the Introduction.

L'AMOUR POUR TOUJOURS

I walked into her front room this afternoon
where she lay resting, very tired,
on her day couch
so she could lie on her left side
and look out at the beach and ocean.
It was mid-August in 2022.
She had been suffering from
the effects of a life-threatening disease.
She did not want harsh chemicals
that would put her in severe pain,
so she was using several alternative protocols
that we had researched and found to be successful,
and that she felt would give her a chance
to follow a gentler route.
She is and always has been a woman of great beauty
and very tall like me, almost as long as
my six and one-half foot frame.
Her high level of intelligence is obvious,
as is her charm.
Poet and performance artist,
musician and song writer,
and to me, best friend and love of my life.
We were born in the same year, war babies.
At the time of this writing we have been together for
Fifty-four and one-half years.
Stuck together gladly, happily.
Married each other at one point.
Partners in many ventures, on many lands,

on a handshake soon after we met
on a rainy night in February, 1968, in L.A.
The magic of how we met is yet another story.
Now, I was worried to distraction about her,
bound to do everything I could to help her,
devoted to her, to help save her from
an end we did not want.
We love each other without limit,
devoted to each other,
trusting each other always.
I quietly approached her bed,
she was lying on her left side,
right leg crossed over her left,
breathing softly.
I figured she was awake
with eyes closed, but not sleeping.
She was dressed only in her undies
and a long tee-shirt.
I softly touched her bottom with my right hand.
She opened her eyes and said her
favorite name for me, Hankie,
a name my Mom had called my Dad.
Sadly she never knew my Dad,
he would have loved her,
he loved poets.
Dad died just a few months before I met her.
As I leaned over her and stared at her,
about to kiss her right cheek,
her long right arm lifted off her side
and she looked up at my face.
She opened her hand and gently put
it on the left side of my face.
Then she turned her head a little backwards
to see my face fully, and said quietly, smiling,
"My wonderful Frank."

I just stared at her.
Neither of us needed to say a word.
She is the wonderful love of my life.
We shall see how this medical journey
we are on in a desperate attempt
to save her life
will go . . .

—Frank Lutz

THE OPTIMIST

As I look at her
the same way other lucky men
have looked at their mates
over time and time again,
I realize her beauty
and kindness,
the glow of who she is
and has been
to me
over all
these
many years,
decades,
are the touchstones
of our attraction
to each other.
It's why I love her so.
It's not about me,
it is about us
and the why
and the how
we came together.
She was and is a gift to
to me.
A soul that brings me
good fortune,
like a compass point,
an azimuth
that
if you follow
it will take you to a place
unimaginable
in its peace
and pleasure.

Just the fact that
she is here,
that she exists
in my world,
and I in hers
are points of reverence
for me,
the good
that I am so fortunate
to know her
and to be near her
for most of my life
for the rest of my life,
and the elemental
truth
that we are now
and always will be
fundamental
to each others' worlds,
and to our own worlds,
as true as the existence
of any lives
in the here and now
or in the past
united by love,
produced by love,
held together
by love.

—*Frank Lutz*

PART II

THE LOVE ACHE

I can't take her anywhere
anymore.
Not out to eat
at her favorite places,
nor to the movies,
nor to the opera,
nor on short trips
like to Santa Barbara,
nor to New York City,
nor to Europe,
nor to Africa,
nor back to Rome
so I can finish
my Vatican project.
I can't even hold her hand anymore.
Before Covid hit
three years ago
we were planning Rome.
Then that plague
infected the world.
But as the worldwide infection
was subsiding,
in April of this year 2022
Linda discovered a lump
in her tummy.
Off to the doctors
and the limits they gave her,
no surgery, no radiation,
only chemotherapy.
And so—she elected not
to suffer incapacitated
if these were to be her

last months with us
who she loved, and who loved her.
There, then started our
six-month journey
with the alternative care folks,
in Mexico and Canada and here.
But in August she was feeling uneasy,
to the extent that she told me
"Hankie, I might not make it,
I might die."
To which I cried out
"No, Linda, you can't die!
I would rather die,
than to see you die!"
To which she cried back,
with wide open eyes
"No, Frank, no—
I could not survive without you.
I would not know what to do!"
I had no response to that,
and only comforted her.
Just before midnight,
on Friday evening, September 2nd,
she was having pains in her tummy,
more than usual.
I took her to UCLA Hospital,
where they admitted her
and made her comfortable,
and took her into a nice room.
This would be her last place to be alive.
We loved each more than words can express,
so on Tuesday afternoon, September 6th,
we got married—for the second time!
But that's a story for another time.

During the week that followed
she worked in the morning constantly
on her computer,
typing new poems and new ideas
for new shows, into September,
October, November—
she was not giving up!
Then on Saturday, Sunday, Monday,
I could tell something different
was happening.
She was getting weaker,
sleeping more,
not working so much
on her beloved computer.
I was exhausted Monday evening
from not eating, not sleeping.
I had tried to sleep
in a very uncomfortable chair
by her bed, the night before,
but to no avail.
So at about 8:30pm
I kissed her on her sleeping head
and went home,
fell asleep in my clothes.
At 4:45am I received a call:
"Mr. Lutz, this is UCLA Hospital
calling you.
I am very sorry to tell you
that your dear wife Linda
has passed away this morning,
at 4:40am . . ."
I had no idea
that her end was so near.
In a daze I drove back to
her room.

She was at peace,
Beautiful, always beautiful.
I kissed her on her forehead
as she lay in her bed.
Then I sat in the chair by her bed,
and took her hand in mine,
and I spoke to her:
"Linda, I will always love you, I will love you forever.
And as Dante followed Virgil when Virgil beckoned
him, when you see my time is near, beckon me
like Virgil beckoned Dante, and I will follow you.
And I will find you again, my Love."

That would be the last time I will see her,
the last time I will hold her hand, until . . .

—*Frank Lutz*

ON THE LIFE OF LINDA J. ALBERTANO

I met Linda on a dark, cold, rainy winter Monday night in February 1968. On this Monday night at just after 6:00pm I had no car, having just recently arrived in L.A. So, I was standing on the curb near the corner of Sunset Blvd. and Doheny Drive, in Beverly Hills, not far from where I had rented a temporary room, hitchhiking with my thumb out toward traffic, and my jacket pulled over my head against the rain. After a few minutes I heard a *"honk-honk"* somewhere behind me, but for some reason I failed to turn around and look; the "duh" channel?

Whoever it was, that person was kind enough to wait a few nanoseconds and this time *"honk-honk-HONK"* to get my attention! So I turned around and saw a long arm sticking out of the passenger window signaling for me to come on to the car. I figured it was a passenger's arm in the window, but when I got to the car and looked inside, the arm belonged to a gorgeous young lady my age who was sitting in the driver's seat. She said, "Come on and get in out of the rain," which I did. She started driving, and as I looked over to see her again, she was tall, very tall like me, and gorgeous. Of course, I forgot all about my meeting with my agent/manager Byron, et al.

Then I said "Hi, my name's Frank. What's yours?" She kept her eyes on the road and said in an easy way "Linda." Next . . . next, I thought to myself, looking in my mind's eye for my next line. Then "Would you like to stop and have a coffee with me?" She quickly responded "No." I had to keep thinking for my next line. But in a few seconds, she said to me "But I'll stop and have tea and cherry soup with you." Tea and cherry soup? Cool! I knew about cherry soup. In between universities in Europe, I worked on a farm in Denmark, where they served cherry soup cold with cream on it for a dessert—really good! So I said "Great! Tea and cherry soup!" Later in our lives together, Linda would tell the story, adding "Frank was the only guy in L.A. who knew about cherry soup."

Then we stopped at a restaurant/bar on Cahuenga Blvd. in Hollywood. She was very easy to talk to over cherry soup, interesting, good-humored, engaging. Neither of us had a phone, and I didn't have a car yet. We exchanged addresses, and I asked if I could come see her the next day. She said "OK" but probably wasn't taking me seriously, because she lived over near Griffith Park, a long stretch through L.A. from Doheny and Sunset where I was staying. I would either have to hitchhike through town, or take the bus, which would be complicated and slow. After cherry soup she dropped me off at my manager's home, and I told her I would see her tomorrow.

The next day, after two hours of hitchhiking through Beverly Hills, West Hollywood, and L.A., I found her street near Griffith Park, just south of Franklin Avenue. She had told me she lived as a tenant in an old three-story house, with a long, wide circular staircase up to the third floor, where she lived in the peaked attic room. When I found the house, I said hello to the maid, and walked in past her and right up the circular staircase to the third floor, to a door. I knocked on the door, and there was Linda!

We spent the day together getting to know each other. We walked through Griffith Park, and that area, and talked about everything art, music, film, theater, and poetry. We talked about politics. We talked about life in general and it was great. We also talked about the fact that she had two part-time jobs and was also teaching guitar part-time. And she was going to film school at UCLA. So I started having a lot of admiration and respect for her because she had no complaints about any of it. Period. That day began the next almost fifty-five years of being happy in life and love partners together.

I always told her that I was the lucky one, but she always told me that she was the lucky one, too. Looking back over the decades, friends have told me that there was a certain magic to our relationship. And something in my background tells me they are right. I will digress for a minute with a little story:

> *When I was about twelve years old, my Dad and I were talking about art. Dad, who was an athlete and a scholar, like I would become, said this to me: "A lot of folks think that music is the highest form of art. But I don't. I think that poetry is the highest form of art."*

> *"Why's that, Dad?"*
>
> *"Because in my mind the point of poetry is to elevate the language, to make it more expressive and beautiful, so that people can better express their feelings and intentions and perceptions of the world. Some poets even bring new words into the language, poets like Shakespeare."*

Dad is where I got my love for poetry. My Dad died just a few months before I met Linda. They never met each other, but they would have loved each other. So, if you think about how Linda and I met—a dark rainy night on Sunset Blvd., early evening traffic, thousands of cars going by—how many of those cars would have had a poet in them? One in ten thousand? A million? And when she honked, and I didn't respond, she had a nanosecond to decide whether to move on, or give it one more try, give me one more chance. So she honked a second time, this time louder and longer, until I got it. When I got into her car, neither she nor I knew that "forever" would be right ahead of us, coming on to include us.

A couple of decades ago, after I had known and been with Linda for over three decades, I was out having lunch with my Chicago buddy, a devout Italian-American Roman Catholic, Tony Gutilla. I was talking about my two favorite subjects: Linda and Dad, how much alike they were in so many ways. Tony did not know Dad, but he knew and loved Linda. He was quiet until I got done. He was looking at me straight in my eyes. Then he said quietly but affirmatively: "Frank, you know what I think—really, what I know? I believe with all my heart that your Dad sent Linda to you as a gift from his grave. He sent her here to look after you because he loved you." Tony's statement astounded me; I had no response to it, but thought it was beautiful.

Since Linda passed away this past September 13, 2022, I have thought a lot about the early sequence of events: the rainy night, the fact that Linda could have kept on driving after the first honking and no response, the fact that she honked louder a second time and did not leave but waited for me, the fact that she was a poet, no doubt the only one in all those cars, and that her family had abandoned her at an early age. No one to trust, no one to rely on. I think Tony was right. I also think that I was sent somehow to look after her, as no one else was there for her. We took to each other early and stayed together happily for over five and one-half decades and were happy to be able to follow our own pursuits—she as a multimedia artist, me as a scholar and commercial pilot—and support each other. The longer time went on, the happier we both were with our lives together.

I also believe that very early on a bond of trust was sealed between us. In September of 1969 Linda had been in the Santa Monica Sears-Roebuck store's hardware department, looking for a part to help brace her Arriflex movie camera that UCLA had loaned her to make her class film. A film that the next year would be voted #1 film of the year at UCLA. As she walked by the batteries table, she put two batteries in her pullover packet, as her hands were full with other stuff. She got arrested for trying to shoplift and was summoned to court. She was very nervous, as she had never been to court before. I knew she did not know how to defend herself. I told her I was going with her. At court I seated us in the first row of seats. When the judge called her up and swore her in, he read the charges against her, and asked her how she would plead. Obviously, "not guilty" and said simply that she did not do that. The judge did not buy her story and told her he could give her fourteen days in jail. At this, I started flailing my hands in the air.

"Who is this?" said the judge. "Do you know him?"

"Yes, your Honor. He's my friend, Frank."

The judge asked me if I wanted to say something, I affirmed, so he told me to stand up, and he swore me in.

"What do you have to say, Mr. Frank?"

I said emphatically "Your Honor, I know this young lady. I know that she is not a thief nor a shoplifter, that she has a high degree of honesty and integrity, and that she would not shoplift anything."

He thought for a minute and responded, "OK. I'll tell you what. I will remand Ms. Albertano into your custody. That means, if either one of you gets out of whack and ends up back in this courtroom, I'll give you both fourteen days in jail. How's that, Mr. Frank?"

I said smiling "OK by me, your Honor. That's fine with me."

Looking back over our lives together, that early incident had created a bond of trust between us that would always be honored, never broken.

In the eighties as the City of L.A. built the Los Angeles Theatre Center, when it was finished, they asked Linda as a prominent performance artist to do the inaugural theater piece there. She wrote, directed, and acted in "Joan of

Compton, Joan of Arcadia," a piece about L.A.'s multi-cultural and financially diverse culture; it got excellent reviews. I did some of the photography for the production. She also did the beautiful "Summertime" piece, a mix of music and poetry, at the John Anson Ford Theatre.

She performed many times in many venues in L.A., such as MOCA and Beyond Baroque, as well as in venues across the USA, Canada, and Europe. Linda and Wanda Coleman represented the USA at the One World Poetry Festival in Amsterdam. She performed with the fabulous Nearly Fatal Women as one of the trio. Linda did two world tours with Alice Cooper as a featured performer on stage in "Nightmare" and "Nightmare 2." She played both the Evil Nurse, and the Executioner. She and the cast received Platinum records for both shows, as the music performance was very popular with fans.

Linda continued to write poetry and do her performance art into the eighties and nineties. During that time, she performed locally at Barnsdall Park, the Wadsworth Theatre, the John Anson Ford Theatre, and many other venues, including the Getty and Royce Hall. She also performed elsewhere in the USA, Canada, and Europe. Linda always got good reviews for her work.

Late in the decade of the 90s we were at a Sunday music festival at Dorsey High School in L.A., where we met for the first time Prince Diabaté, the great Kora (or Cora) player from Guinea, West Africa. Linda took to the music and instrument, and thus began a wonderful relationship between Prince and us. Early in the present century we visited Guinea, on two occasions, so that Linda could study the Kora and other West African musical instruments. She became a part of Prince's ensemble and played in several venues with his group, or just as a duo with Prince, for two decades. I am also proud to say that we facilitated Prince's becoming a citizen of the USA.

In 2001, Linda was one of five poets inducted and inscribed into the famous Venice Poets' Wall Monument on Venice Beach; her name and some of her poetry was put into the cement wall, reminiscent of Homer, and is there for all to see.

More recently, Linda had been writing poetry and making occasional appearances before she died. Before COVID three years ago, I had planned to return to the Vatican to follow-up on a long-term research project I have been doing and take Linda with me. (I have a Vatican Passport.) We had been to Rome before, of course, and she loved Italy anyway. But alas, the dreaded

COVID curtailed a lot of travel. Then on April 7, 2022, early in the morning, Linda discovered a lump on her tummy. We went right into action, seeking both conventional and alternative therapy. We also went to Mexico, where we had sought medical treatment for a malignant breast tumor in 1987, which was successful.

That battle we won, and Linda lived for thirty-five more years. She actually went on an Alice Cooper tour during that time, too. This time was different. We had been working hard, seven days per week with various therapies, to save her. Tests here and in Mexico showed that her cancer had already metastasized. Her last few months were full of desperation and hope, love, and laughs, and her always sweet and cheerful smile, and great sense of humor, and poetry presentations in venues. She was very brave.

But at one point less than two months before she died, we were sitting together talking when she said to me "Hankie, I think I might not make it. I think I might die." I was shocked and jumped to my feet, exclaiming "No, Linda, you can't die! I would rather die than you!" She looked back at me, with her eyes wide open big, almost fearful, and said "No, Frank, you can't die before me! If you die, I wouldn't know how to take care of myself! I wouldn't be able to survive!" I was stunned, but silent. I could only kneel down by her chair and put my arm around her. Then she said "When we are girls and young women, we are always taught to palpate our breasts, but they never mention our tummies. But we should palpate our tummies, too. Maybe we would have caught this sooner." Sometime later, in the hospital at UCLA Santa Monica, she told me she did not think she would make it beyond the next couple of weeks: "But I will be at peace, Frank. It's those who live on who suffer the most." And that is true, by my own account.

On the morning of Tuesday, September 6, I was at home when I got a call from our dear friend and tax accountant for over forty-five years, Larry Johnson. Larry had called several times, always worried about Linda, who he loved. We were talking calmly, when suddenly he blurted out "Frank, you guys gotta get married!" He was not usually so excitable and emphatic. I said "But Larry! We did get married a couple of decades ago, don't you remember? We did that CDP thing, the California Domestic Partnership!" "No, no Frank, I mean, really married, like a real wedding marriage!" Anyway, he calmed down, sent both Linda and me his love, and I headed for UCLA Hospital in Santa Monica.

I entered Linda's room at about 1:30pm. For some reason, the word "married" was in the air—one of us, either Linda or I, said the word "married," like Linda, Larry and I were all on the same brain wave. I don't know what happened, but I said "Linda, should we get married?" And she said "Yes!"

The next thing I knew, I was on my cell phone, and I Googled "Justice of the Peace who can perform a marriage." An 818 number came up, and I called it; a man answered it.

"Hi. Can you do marriages?"

"Yes, sure, I am certified, I have the license, and notary stamp. Why?"

"I, we, want to get married."

"When?"

"This afternoon?"

"This afternoon? OK. Where are you?"

I gave him directions. I recognized his accent, as I grew up in a wonderful Jewish neighborhood, so I heard Russia and Israel in his voice. I am not Jewish, but I love them, and thought when I was younger, if I ever get married, I want to do that with a Rabbi. I then called my French buddy Jean Caby, who lives a few minutes from UCLA Hospital.

"Do you want to witness Linda and me getting married this afternoon, for the second time?"

"Hell yes, absolutely!"

Jean showed up in one-half hour with a huge bouquet of flowers for Linda. At 4:15pm the Rabbi showed up, a big guy named Josh, with a friendly face and demeanor. He spoke: "OK. So now we have to take 25 minutes to fill out this paperwork, after which I will give you the license."

After we filled out and signed the documents, Josh said "OK. Now we are gonna have the marriage rites and ceremony. So Frank, you get over beside Linda's bed, and kneel down beside her."

He then proceeded, "Frank, do you take Linda to be your lawful wedded wife..."

And then Linda, "Linda, do you..."

After the respective "I do" iterations from Linda and me, and a few "rules" of marriage from Josh, he finally said "Frank, you may kiss the bride. Now you are officially married, congratulations!"

I kissed Linda, and we both cried like babies. Tears of joy. It was the happiest moment for both of our lives, truly. Jean Caby has it all in photos, thankfully.

On the evening of September 12, I had been up for about forty-eight hours, running back and forth to the hospital, unable to sleep or eat, worried about the Love of my Life. I went home at 8pm, exhausted, and fell asleep in my clothes. At 4:45 am on Tuesday, September 13, my cell phone rang.

"Hello."

"Mr. Lutz, this is UCLA Hospital calling you. I am very sorry to tell you that your dear wife Linda has passed away this morning, at 4:40am."

In her room, I sat beside her bed, and took her hand in mine. She was at peace, thin, but still beautiful. This would be the last time I would ever see her. Until... Some days before she died, I told her something that I would now repeat to her, after she died. "Linda, I will always love you, I will love you forever. And as Dante followed Vergil when Vergil beckoned him, when you see my time is near, beckon me like Vergil beckoned Dante, and I will follow you. And I will find you again, my Love."

—***Frank A. Lutz***
co-author, editor, husband

Linda, during her six decades in various art disciplines, won awards and recognition in poetry, performance art, music and film, including the rare title of Poetry Diva from the City of Los Angeles.

EPILOGUE

Over the years—decades—people have asked me about Linda, her background, where she is from, how we met, and so forth.

Linda J. Albertano had her first poem published in the early 1960s in Orange County, California when she was nineteen years old. During the following sixty-one years, she would develop prominence in poetry, performance art, music, and film. She performed and worked her arts in the USA and other parts of the Western Hemisphere, Europe, and Africa. The number of venues, theaters, and stadiums where she performed, plus small clubs and private showings, can be counted in the hundreds. Her poems were published in dozens of magazines and poetry anthologies.

Linda spent the first eight years of her life with her family in Utah, Montana, and finally Denver. At age eight, when her brother Jim was only four years old, their father abandoned the family and accused their mother Alberta of not being able to care for the children, which was untrue. This is just one reason Linda's support for Women's Rights was unwavering throughout her career in all of her art disciplines.

Alberta was a fine person. Very loving of her children and an artist, as Linda would become. Linda always said, "Any good qualities I have, I got from my mother."

Her father reported Alberta to Denver child "welfare," who took the children and put them into foster homes, and worse, separated them into different homes! Both Linda and her brother Jim would be treated to several years of neglect and abuse in the foster homes, which would have a negative impact on them for the rest of their lives.

Linda was often not allowed to eat meals with the foster family and treated more like a domestic maid than a child. Linda went on to become an Honors student both in high school and in college at University of Colorado, Boulder. At age nineteen her father remarried, and her step-mother refused to fund Linda's

University of Colorado tuition or expenses. (Contrary to some misinformation about her, Linda was born on April 17, 1942, and not 1952.)

So her weak-minded father gave her $50.00 in spending money and a one-way ticket to Los Angeles, where Linda knew no one! Linda struggled in L.A., doing odd jobs until she was discovered due to her beauty and height, when she started to work doing modeling and some TV work, including as a regular friend of *The Monkees* on their TV program, as well as the TV show, *Ozzie and Harriet*.

For a time, she was also the Space Girl at Disneyland, and she appeared in the movies *Mary Poppins* and *Beach Red*, an Academy Award nominated film. She was also developing her talent as a guitar-playing Blues singer. Linda Ronstadt and The Stone Poneys and Taj Mahal recorded at least one of Linda's Blues songs called "2:10 Train" on one of their albums. During the mid-1960s Linda made two trips with the USO during the Vietnam War as a dancer-singer with an all-girls troupe to Vietnam, Cambodia, Thailand, South Korea, and Japan.

In 1966 she enrolled at UCLA to complete her higher education and get a degree. Because of her excellent grades, obvious intelligence, and lack of family support, UCLA gave Linda a grant and scholarship money to attend that great university. Her Senior Class film was voted by students and faculty in the Film Department the Best Film of the Year when she graduated in 1971.

When I met Linda she had no family support, nor help from anyone else. She did all of this on her own.

It is also interesting to note that Linda Albertano was the first female member of Gold's Gym, Venice, having joined in 1970 when she was in UCLA film school, to get her arms stronger for carrying heavy camera equipment.

—*FL*

PART II

POSTSCRIPT

A fact that I did not include in this story about Linda is that I had been writing poetry for several years before we met in 1968. I started writing poetry in the early 1960s during my time sailing with the Woods Hole Oceanographic Institution in Massachusetts as a student scientist. I sailed on the RV Atlantis and then on the RV Atlantis II, around the globe. I also was writing poetry during my time in 1964 at the University of Perugia in Italy, as well as when I was in school in France and Germany. Linda had read my poetry many times and loved it. I wrote about war, flying (I have a commercial pilot's license), history, and mystical events that have come to me in my dreams. But with Linda I never pushed to perform my poetry, because I did not want her to think that I was competing with her, or encroaching on her intellectual territory, so close to home. So I stayed in the background and supported her and her efforts. She deserved my support in all parts of her life. So the fact of our meeting on that cold, dark, rainy February night in 1968 when she stopped to pick me up from hitchhiking looms even larger in our fates.

The conversation with my Dad about the importance of poetry (his own Master's Thesis was on the US Civil War and the great American poet Robert Frost); the thousands of cars going by me on the streets that night when she stopped for me; her decision to wait for me and to honk again, more aggressively; the fact that she was a poet. How many other cars that night could have had such a rare person as a poet in them? And the fact that I was, still am, a poet. My buddy Tony Gutilla had it right: Linda was my Dad's gift to me from his grave. But she considered me to be a gift to her, too, from someone, maybe some ancestor, who cared for her.

So the proof is "in the pudding" so they say: fifty-five years together, through good times and hard times. I have been told many times that our relationship was "meant to be." Yes, I agree. Linda told me that our relationship was preordained.

What do you think Reader? . . . email me at FrankALutz@gmail.com

—FL

PART III

Welcome to the Life of

Linda J. Albertano

BEYOND BAROQUE

681 Venice Boulevard, Venice, CA 90291 • Ph: (310) 822-3006   Fax (310) 827-7432

LITERARY ARTS CENTER

11, 18 September, Thursdays - 8:30 PM

NEARLY FATAL WOMEN

Two more nights of this fall's run from Los Angeles' hottest poetry/performance divas. Poet SUZANNE LUMMIS, musician and performance artist ANNA HOMLER, poet LAUREL ANN BOGEN, and performance artist/poet LINDA ALBERTANO deliver their fiery cool and noir mischief, in an evening of adult fun, Nearly Fatal classics and new materials. Don't miss this astonishing group as it combines poetry, performance art, visual theater, humor, and pure Los Angeles brilliance, and before their widely anticipated New York debut.

Anna Homler in absentia Thursday, sept. 18th

General Admission: $7. $5 students & seniors. Members free!
We are located on Venice Blvd. 3/4 of a mile west of Lincoln Blvd. on the north side, in the Old Venice Town Hall.

GET INVOLVED IN BEYOND BAROQUE. BE PART OF THE ACTION!

**Beyond Baroque
& MOCA present**

Frank O'Hara's
The General

Performed by

Kenward Elmslie
&
Linda Albertano

with

Michael Silverblatt
Ellyn Maybe
Jeff McDaniel
Ryan Oba

3 PM in the MOCA Auditorium   10/31/1999

ALLEN GINSBERG'S AMERICA

A MEMORIAL TRIBUTE and CELEBRATION

Proceeds to benefit the NAROPA INSTITUTE

...in person...

LINDA ALBERTANO
WILLIAM BURROUGHS
EXENE CERVENKOVA
THE DARK BOB
FIRESIGN THEATER
THE FUGGS
GARTH HUDSON
LEWIS MAC ADAMS
JACK NICHOLSON
RED HOT CHILI PEPPERS
MARTIN SHEEN
KURT VONNEGUT, JR.
ANNE WALDMAN

...and more!!!

Hosted by Ed Sanders and Paul Krasner

Saturday, June 21, 1997 - 7pm (doors open 6:30)

WADSWORTH THEATER - Westwood

Tickets Available thru TICKETMASTER (213) 480-3232 or
UCLA Ticket Office (310) 825-2101

Produced by Rhino Records, L.A. Weekly and Jerry Moss

Linda J. Albertano, *Summertime*, performance, John Anson Ford Theater.
Photograph: Basia Kenton

I.R.S. RECORDS PRESENTS

THE CUTTING EDGE

MUSIC, INTERVIEWS, EDUCATION

This month: Performance and interview with LONE JUSTICE, LOVE TRACTOR, STEEL PULSE recounts the making of the film BACHELOR PARTY, poet LINDA ALBERTANO. All hosted by the beady-eyed sun-bronzed surf cat, PETER ZAREMBA with his sandy friends. YOWZA!

Sunday, June 24 9 p.m. PDST
12 midnight EDST

MTV MUSIC TELEVISION

Just what the world needs, another rock show.
© 1984 International Record Syndicate, Inc.

I.R.S.

Cactus Foundation
P.O. Box 36422
L.A., CA 90036

LINDA J. ALBERTANO
IN
ALICE COOPER'S "NIGHTMARE 11"

UNITED KINGDOM TOUR

NOV. 23 WEMBLEY, ENGLAND
NOV. 25 EDINBURGH, SCOTLAND
NOV. 26 EDINBURGH, SCOTLAND
NOV. 28 MANCHESTER, ENGLAND
NOV. 29 MANCHESTER, ENGLAND
NOV. 30 MANCHESTER, ENGLAND
DEC. 1   NEWCASTLE, ENGLAND
DEC. 3   BIRMINGHAM, ENGLAND
DEC. 4   BIRMINGHAM, ENGLAND
DEC. 5   BIRMINGHAM, ENGLAND

Photo Philip Murray

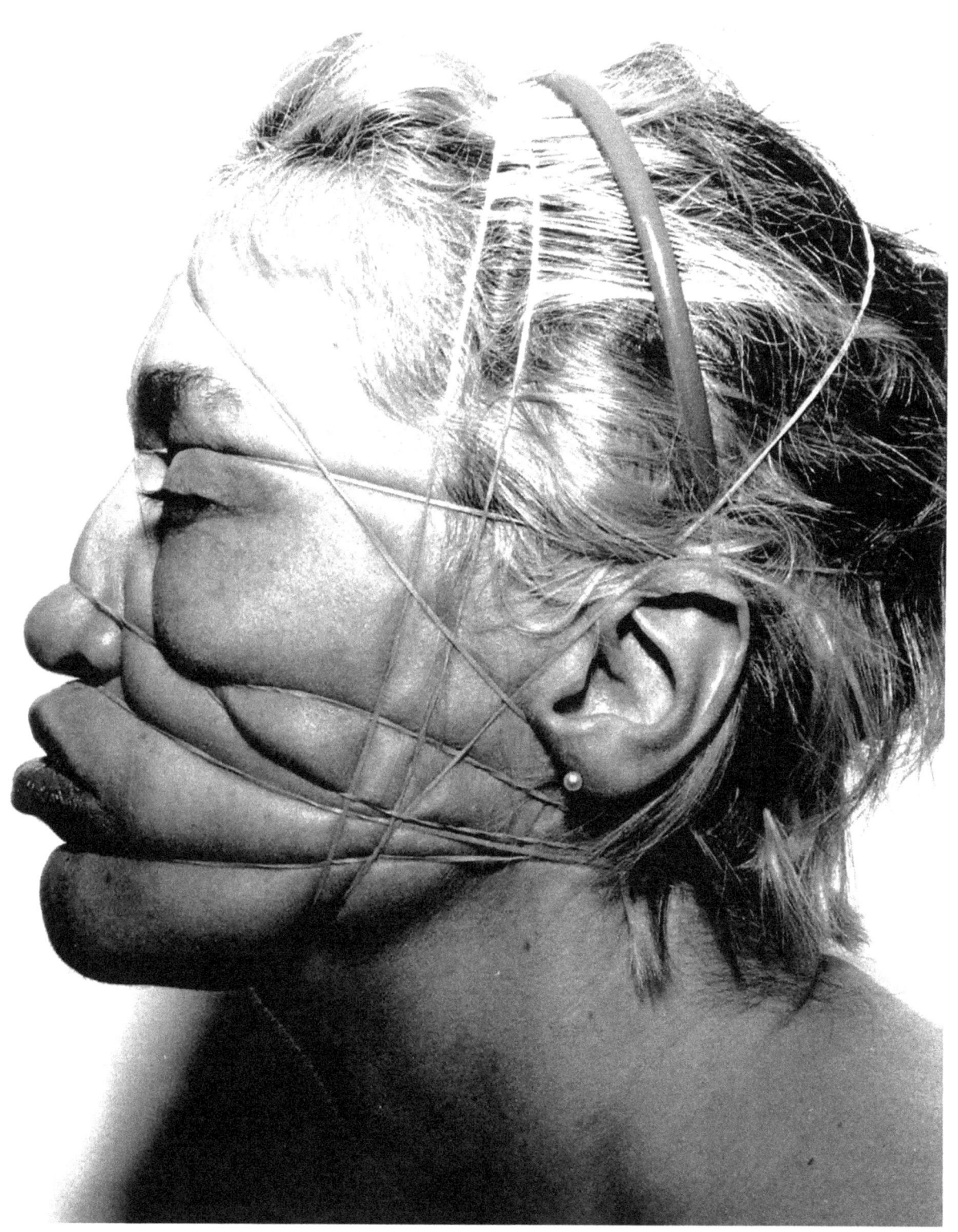

THREE ROOMS PRESS presents

SCUM
THE VALERIE SOLANAS STORY

APRIL 29, 2018
BEYOND BAROQUE | VENICE, CALIFORNIA

written by **Kat Georges**

directed by **Peter Carlaftes**

Starring (in order of appearance)

Linda J. Albertano	Dorothy
Dawn Walters	Vivian
Christian Georgescu	Golem
S. A. Griffin	Bernard
Bibiana Padilla Maltos	Valerie Solanas

Tech Master: Richard Modiano | Honorary Stage Manager: Neil "Skooter" Taylor
Running time is approximately 60 minutes with no intermission.
Please turn off all electronics before curtain. No photos or videos are permitted. Thank you!

Production Notes: I was introduced to Valerie Solanas' infamous work, *The S.C.U.M. Manifesto*, in the early 1990s and was consumed by the comic brilliance of her writing. How could this oddball genius succumb to shooting (and almost killing) pop art superstar Andy Warhol on June 3, 1968? Research led to the discovery that one of Solanas' main motivations for attacking Warhol was that he had allegedly promised to produce her original play, cleverly titled, *Up Your Ass*. On learning this, I immediately decided that she would be a great character for a play.

After shooting Warhol, Solanas was indicted and by August was sent to a mental hospital while awaiting trial. Somehow, for three days around Christmas of that year, she was let out of the hospital on bail (apparently paid for by an anonymous rich man). Warhol spent those three days riding around Manhattan in a limo and refusing to get out. I started by determining that the play would be set in a party hosted at The Factory during this time, and would be filled with Warhol superstars, all waiting for Warhol to show up. Instead, they get Valerie—and her mother—and all hell breaks loose.

I wrote and rewrote the play several times, but I wasn't satisfied. It didn't capture the madness of the era: the chaos, the crazed drug-infused sparkle, the breaking of all standards of the past. In frustration, I ripped up the first scene, ready to start writing again. But something happened. I glanced at the ripped up pages and started repositioning the pieces. Characters' dialogue was broken up and rearranged. It no longer made linear sense, but it had the energy I needed. I screamed and grabbed a pair of scissors and cut every page of the script into strips, cut monologues into pieces, grabbed some tape and fastened things together in a new order. It worked on the page. On the stage it was one of the most successful productions, reprised twice at San Francisco's Marilyn Monroe Memorial Theater.

WHO'S WHO

Linda J. Albertano *(Dorothy)* is a musician, storyteller, and performance artist whose work has been presented in Europe as well as America. A long-time Venice resident, she has been featured frequently at Beyond Baroque, SPARC, LACE, Highways, and other literary/spoken word meccas.

Dawn Walters *(Vivian)* Born and raised in Northern California, Dawn performed in her first play at the age of six. Today, she is an LA-based actress, licensed court reporter, amateur jazz dancer, and animal lover. She has a Bachelor of Arts degree in Russian and has lived in Poland and Northern Ireland. Notable films include *Artistic License* (2005) and *Parthenabe* (2007).

Christian Georgescu *(Golem)* is a writer, performer, and visual artist from New York City. Graduate of Pratt Institute and American Academy of Dramatic Arts East, Rob McCaskill Studio NY. His acclaimed solo performance work, *House of Me*, was recently featured in festivals in New York and Los Angeles.

S. A. Griffin *(Bernard)* is an award-winning poet, actor, performance artist, editor, and publisher who lives, loves and works in Los Angeles. Traveled the U.S. and Canada with The Carma Bums, and is the visionary behind The Poetry Bomb. In 2011 he became the first person to receive Beyond Baroque Literary Art Center's Distinguished Service Award.

Bibiana Padilla Maltos *(Valerie Solanas)* is a writer and conceptual artist closely tied to the Fluxus lifestyle. Her artistic work includes collage and the reinvention of performances and classic metadramas, as well as the exploration of visual narratives parallel to literary and political texts, as well as the explorations of the body's sense in contemporary societies.

Peter Carlaftes *(director)* is a New York-based author, playwright, and performer. Former co-artistic director of San Francisco's Marilyn Monroe Memorial Theater where he wrote and directed 15 plays including *ANTI*, *Spin-Dry*, *Closure*, and *Inside Straight*. In New York, he has written and starred in *Lenny Bruce: Dead and Well*, a solo performance piece, *Dueling Karaoke*, *Greenagers in Love*, and *Sarah's Choice*. He is co-director of Three Rooms Press.

Kat Georges *(playwright)* wrote and directed 15 plays during her tenure as co-artistic director of San Francisco's Marilyn Monroe Memorial Theater. In New York since 2003, she has directed numerous Off-Broadway plays (including *The Old In and Out* by Madeline Artenberg and Karen Hildebrand, *Twitter Theater*, *Jack Kerouac: Catholic* and *Memo from Allen Ginsberg*, by Larry Myers, and *Sarah's Choice* by Peter Carlaftes. Her books include the full-length poetry collection, *Our Lady of the Hunger*, and, most recently, *Three Somebodies: Plays About Notorious Dissidents*. A longtime graphic designer, she is co-director of Three Rooms Press.

Special Thanks to Richard Modiano for his continuing visionary leadership at Beyond Baroque, and, in particular, his work with lighting, sound, and gracious support of this production. As Beyond Baroque celebrates its 50th anniversary this year, we salute its unique mission as an internationally-renowned venue dedicated to the possibilities of language

Los Angeles Theatre Center
Bill Bushnell, Artistic Producing Director
presents in Theatre 4

LINDA J. ALBERTANO

JOAN OF COMPTON

JOAN OF ARCADIA

INTERMEDIA PERFORMANCE SERIES

Producer, Intermedia Performance Series: **Adam Leipzig**
Coordinator: **Cornell Coley**
Production Stage Manager: **Bill Swadley**
Lighting Designer: **Kathy A. Perkins**
Props: **Margaret Michon-Chadsey, Mary Garber**
Costumes: **Carol Booton**
Video: **Paul Michon-Chadsey**
Audio: **Linda J. Albertano, Philip Murray**
Stage Managers: **Linda Brown & Kristen Kelly**
Light Board Operator: **Rick Yatman**
Sound Operator: **Hunt Burdick**
Technical Director: **David MacMurtry**
Master Electrician: **Todd A. Jared**

Performance: Thursday, March 6 - Sunday,
March 9, 1986. SIX PERFORMANCES ONLY.

While at UCLA, **Linda J. Albertano** read Marx, liked it, and yet remained undaunted in her drive to become a card carrying member of the middle-class. She emerged from college with a BFA in filmmaking and a penchant for singing in sleezy Valley joints with the company of a crazed piano player and a skinny trombonist, who was Kid Ory all over again. She increasingly appeared in exhilarating and abstract productions like Lin Hixson's *Swayback* and *Rockefeller Center*. Plunging recklessly onward, she soon began performing in galleries including LACE in Los Angeles, Sushi in San Diego, and New Langton Arts in San Francisco. She also accosted audiences in clubs with such unlikely names as At My Place, Hop Singh's, Club Lingerie, and The Lhasa. She performed *Pointed Sweethearts* and *Mercenary Children* at the Pilot Theatre and has been featured at Beyond Baroque and Sparc -- two hotbeds of literary activity in Venice, California. In June of 1984 she appeared in *The Cutting Edge, MTV Los Angeles,* and read at The One World Poetry Festival in Amsterdam. She is currently working on a spoken-word album produced by Harvey Kubernik and Ethan James. Albertano's *Greatest Hits* (released by High Performance Audio) is available in the Grand Lobby.

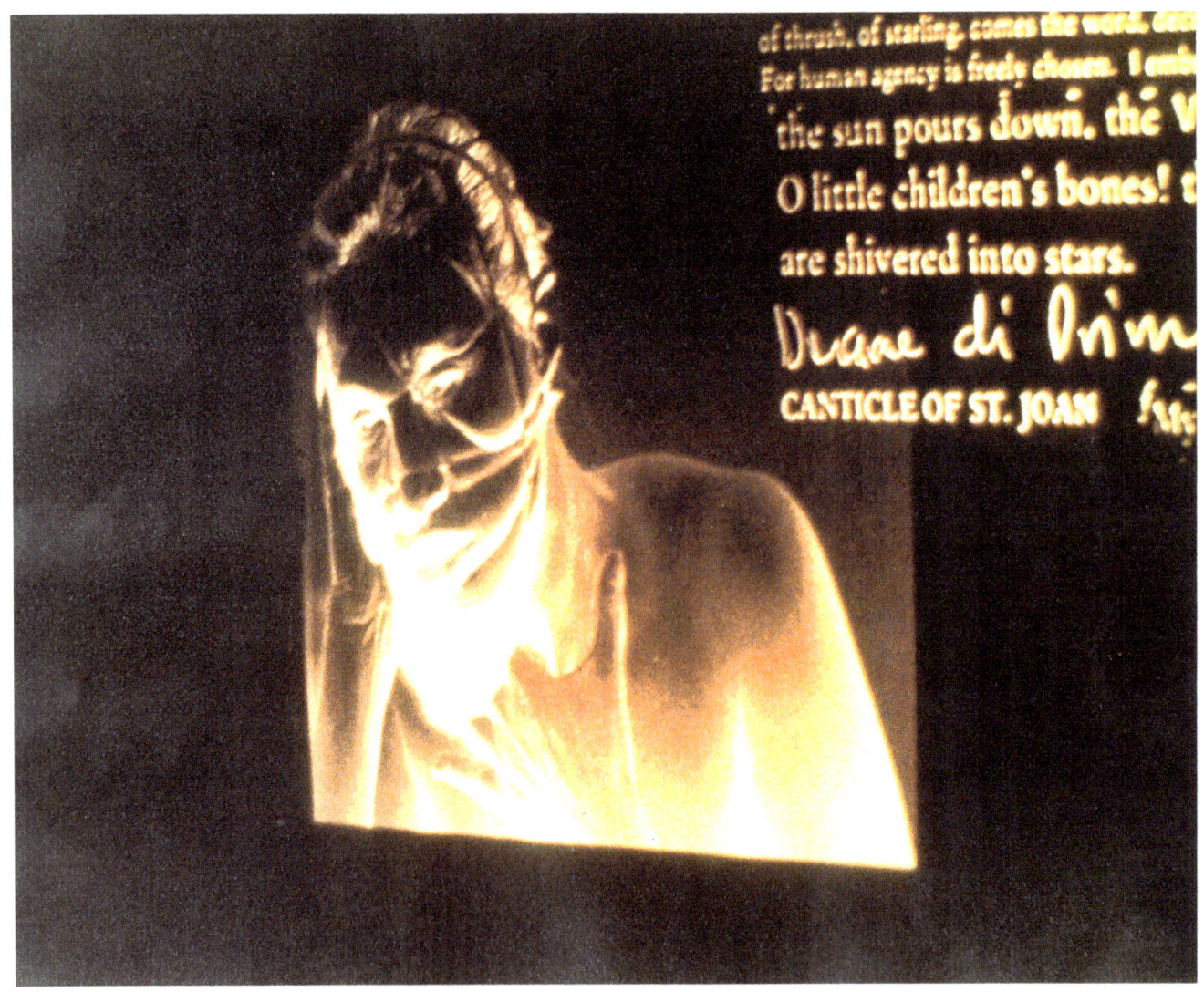

6 THURSDAY

The LA Rhythmettes, a South Los Angeles youth drum corp and drill team, are featured in a new performance work by Linda Albertano, who has incorporated them into her piece, **"Joan of Compton; Joan of Arcadia."** In this performance, she creates a montage of verbal, musical, and visual images exploring white privilege, liberal guilt, and racial alienation. Appearing in this art performance with Albertano and the Rhythmettes will be Wanda Coleman, Ken Ransom, Tequila Mockingbird, Tobi Redlich, Joy Grdnic, and others. The show—part of the Los Angeles Theater Center's opening season Intermedia Performance Series—runs through the 9th. Performances are at 8:00 p.m. with Sat. and Sun. matinees at 2:00 p.m. At 514 S. Spring St., L.A. Tickets are $6. For reservations or information call 627-5599.

New from HIGH PERFORMANCE AUDIO

LINDA J. ALBERTANO
Greatest Hits
Lake Mexia (Tex-Mex) / Lake Mexia (Gregorian) / Crime / Dante's Inferno Blues / Dear Diary / Freud's Slipper Shuffle / Jane, Jane / Atomic Blues

Linda Albertano really respects tradition, but she's not afraid to experiment. Side one draws on popular forms in song and spoken word with lyrics by such notables as Lin Hixson, J.P. Kovacs, Charles Duncan and Albertano herself. Side two is a minimal vocal symphony combining rural song, urban gospel and prose. Plus a jazz-blues with lyrics by the aforementioned Kovacs.

$10 Running Time: 27 mins. 17 secs.

Other cassettes available from HIGH PERFORMANCE AUDIO

MICHAEL PEPPE
Frenzy is Serenity
Soundtrack for an Imaginary Videotape / Adolescent / City / Ad / Thirty-nine Characters / Hands Caught in a Machine

$10

CARTESIAN REUNION MEMORIAL ORCHESTRA
Shadow Boy / Red Fish on Television / The Swing / I can't get no fulfilment / Orlando, he dead / Shakeout / Message for Garcia / Nea Praxis / Law and Order

$10

JACKI APPLE
Free Fire Zone
The Garden Planet Revisited

$14

ANNA HOMLER
Breadwoman
EE CHÈ / OŌ NU DAH / GU SHE' NA' DI / GIYAH / YESH' TE

$10

Send check or money order plus $1.50 for postage and handling to High Performance Audio, 240 S. Broadway, 5th Floor, Los Angeles, CA 90012

POETRY FLASH
P.O. Box 4172
Berkeley, CA 94704

Number 142   *January* 1985

The Bay Area's Poetry Calendar & Review

Amsterdam Poetry Festival '84

☐   HAROLD NORSE

One World Poetry Festival, Amsterdam, Holland, November 2-11, 1984.

THE CANALS NEVER LOOKED GREENER. THE amber glow of the street lamps and their reflections in the water never looked more soothing. The old handsome buildings never looked handsomer. And, despite the season, the weather was mild, with even a spot of sunshine now and then, slant and polar. Some 60 poets from some 20 countries jetted, hitched, motored, pullmanned and broomsticked to the cool, gray Venice of the North.

Because of the jet-lag and chronic insomnia, I missed the first 3 evenings, but made the Los Angeles evening and what looked to me like a Bacchanalian finale the last night of the ten-day bash, held at the Milky Way in the heart of town, where all the youth go to the cafes and night spots. The poetry festival, when one considers the general indifference to poetry in most countries, reaches a large number of people in Amsterdam. In 1978 there were only four or five evenings, which were mostly subdued, with typically small audiences of poets, except for the last night at the Paradiso — a vast multi-leveled combination dancehall, cafe and theatre — where literally thousands showed up, young, boisterous, explosive, beer-drinking and pot-smoking. They did not come for me or for Burroughs, that's certain, although we both read. They came for one of Burroughs' adoring fans, Patti Smith. I remember being sullen and angry — why do rock and punk stars who are *influenced* by poets and novelists get these monster turnouts, and the financial rewards that go with them? We all know the answer to that. (Before he was picked up by rock, punk and New Wave, Burroughs did not draw the way he does now. When he got to the stage, I heard a young German ask, in a thick accent, "Who is this guy?" "Oh, I dunno, some kinda writer, " said his friend in a bored voice. "When does Patti Smith come on?" Burroughs' performance did not bring down the house. The audience talked loudly throughout most of our readings, including his. For Patti Smith they went wild.)

I thought her work was sloppy, pretentious, mannered, derivative. It was full of ostentatious effects, unassimilated influences from Artaud and Rimbaud, diluted cliches. Yet, in the end, to my own dismay, I found myself admitting that for all this she had an unmistakable way with words that generates tingles of excitement. But — it was terrific performance poetry. And this genre had not yet come into its own in 1978.

But in 1984 performance poetry was a poetic genre to conjure with. And it looks like Patti Smith was a precursor; then Laurie Anderson. And at the Festival this year the women took all the gold in this vein. These were the L.A. poets: Linda Albertano, Lydia Lunch and Exene Cervenka. The latter two ladies have the tough, foul-mouthed, streetwise realism of talented punkers who know how to wring every theatrical nuance from mood, language, scene and theme. I don't know how long I'd stay with it on the page, but it was music to my ears. Their voices and bodies the only instruments, they fine-tuned their performance with resources of pitch, tone and volume that makes language jump, gesture and bounce. And they did this without literary pretentiousness in cynical, gutsy raps together. The audience lapped it up. William Carlos Williams would have loved them. They used the American language with a vengeance — brash, glitzy, sassy, mean.

Linda Albertano, on the other hand, a very tall, striking blonde with fine eyes, was softer, more modulated, with a genuine avant-garde cafe style. She gave a riveting performance of monologues in an equally tough vernacular. Wanda Coleman, an imposing, statuesque black poet, did not bring enough originality and surprise to her work, which depended heavily on the familiar rhetoric of social anger and outrage, not enough in itself to make effective poetry, relying on an emotional stance to do the work of language. But she had some powerful moments, especially at the end, where her performance and the text seemed to burst out and grip the listener by sheer force of magic. The men of the L.A. evening didn't do so well, so I'd rather skip over them. The women definitely won this meet, thumbs down.

I don't want to gloss over the Dutch poets, who appeared at several of the evenings as well as their own Dutch evening, which I missed. Simon Vinkenoog, who appeared for some mysterious reason with the LA poets, is the bad boy of Dutch poetry, a prolific rebel poet, translator, performer, impresario and international catalyst for experimental work. Bert Schierbeek is also well-known to readers outside Holland. William Levy, an American who lives and writes in Amsterdam, was in the sixties an editor and publisher of such zeitgeist small press publications as the *International Times, Suck* and *The Fanatic.* Eddie Woods, another American expatriate, runs the English-language little magazine and press, *Ins & Outs,* and is himself a poet of remarkable talent and skill with, at his best, the qualities of a Blaise Cendrars brought to contemporary uses, as in his tour de force, "Ode To The Clap" with its sardonic inscription: *with special thanks to the contributors.*

The Amsterdam Festival is, as far as I know, the only major international forum for experimental poetry in the world, serving the indispensable function of keeping alive the tradition of the New, the non-academic approach in an art form that falls, for the most part, into conservative, conventional modes. The heavy representation of North Americans attests to the viability of the New American poetry that began with Pound and Williams, leading to the Beats with a nod to Cendrars and Apollinaire, and continuing into the present irreverent, very much alive expansion into postmodern surrealism, cut-up, open field, aleatory and performance poetry. I found the whole Amsterdam experience exhilarating.☐

Harold Norse's most recent book of poems is Mysteries of Magritte. *His letter exchange with William Carlos Williams will appear shortly in* Helix *magazine.*

A couple of years back, it seemed that every third car on Melrose had a bumper sticker that read "Linda Albertano ♥ Your Boyfriend." The masses must have been relieved to learn that the sticker advertised a Lhasa show — if the sultry, statuesque performance artist *really* wanted your boyfriend, you'd be out of luck, honey.

Linda Albertano moans, croons and sways her way through a set, sometimes accompanied by a tinny little drum machine and sometimes by her backup group, the Eligible Bachelors. Her work resembles songs, tiny pieces on modern love that cut like a knife; mini political extravaganzas that would convince even the prez to stop doing her wrong. "I'm not the kind of person with the patience to write a novel," she says. "Two and a half minutes seems like just the right length."

She graduated from UCLA's film school with the romantic notion that she'd make enough money waitressing to finance her first film. Disabused of *that* idea rather quickly, she fell in with an arty crowd, began studies with performance diva Rachel Rosenthal and sang with a local ragtime band. Her early work, devastating portraits of bad boyfriends in words and music, was performed in seedy new-wave hellholes like the Lhasa and the Anticlub to small but appreciative audiences. More recent appearances, more focused and political, have been at the Wallenboyd and the John Anson Ford Theater. Earlier this year, a performance for LATC's intermedia series included slides, video, the Rhythmettes (a 30-piece drum corps from Compton) and nearly a dozen musicians. Although all six shows were sold out, they were seen primarily by theatergoers, and ignored by the arty club denizens who'd previously formed the bulk of her audience. "I'd like to expose what I do to a lot more people, people that *we* might not think are the hippest, but who are affected just as much by the work," she says.

While two-thirds of the performance artists in New York seemingly come to Hollywood and the Industry (Laurie Anderson, Spalding Gray, Eric Bogosian), Albertano, ironically, wants nothing to do with film. "When I'm in the company of actors, I don't feel that I'm with my own kind." She's even wary of her own limited success. "I get too nervous about new work, now that I'm better known." For the time being, we must be content to catch her minimalist cabaret of the absurd where we can, at theaters and at poetry readings.

— Hubert Mensch

SKIN

LINDA J. ALBERTANO

BEYOND BAROQUE

681 venice blvd.
venice, california
310.822.3006

18 December, Saturday - 7:30 PM
PRINCE DIABATE and LINDA J. ALBERTANO

A night of kora and poetry.

PRINCE DIABATE is a direct descendent of the Mandingo griots who are the oral historians, storytellers, and living encyclopedias of West African Culture. Prince Diabate has been recognized as one of the greatest living virtuosos of the kora (West African Harp).

LINDA J. ALBERTANO is a musician and spoken-word artist who has recently returned from Conakry, Guinea where she studied kora, bolon, and n'goni (stringed calabash instruments) with Prince Diabate and other masters of ancient musical traditions.

admission: $7 seniors and students: $5 members: free
photo: Habibou Sissoko

CALENDAR

POP REVIEW

LINDA ALBERTANO IN HER OWN RIGHT

Los Angeles Times — Saturday, December 31, 1983 ★

Unfair though it may be, all female performance artists who accompany themselves electronically are in the shadow of Laurie Anderson at the moment. Linda Albertano has much in common with Anderson, yet she managed to carve out a niche of her own during her appearance at the Lhasa Club Thursday. A statuesque singer with a clear, strong voice, Albertano is a warmer, more accessible performer than Anderson, and the humor in her work is much broader.

In a brief variety show that incorporated poetry, a capella vocals, dance and comedy monologue, Albertano addressed the subjects of body building, Catholicism, holiday depression, compulsive busyness and the life of the eligible bachelor. Albertano's central charm is the fact that her take on all these subjects is refreshingly free of rancor and bitterness. In between these bits, she performed (to taped accompaniment) renditions of "Mean to Me," "Summertime" and "Hang On Sloopy" that were strangely stylized to the point of satire. Ultimately, however, Albertano's peculiar singing style is more beautiful than it is funny.

—KRISTINE McKENNA

THE BEST OF L.A.

Best Poetry Entrepreneur
True believer Harvey Kubernik has worked the scene since the late '60s, documenting L.A.'s staggering diversity on three '80s LPs: *Voices of the Angels*, *English as a Second Language* and *Neighborhood Rhythms*. With partner David Barmack, BarKubCo, his new music/spoken-word incarnation, will debut *Hollyword*, a monster cassette and CD projected for late fall featuring "real" and celebrity poets.

The Best Words

By Wanda Coleman

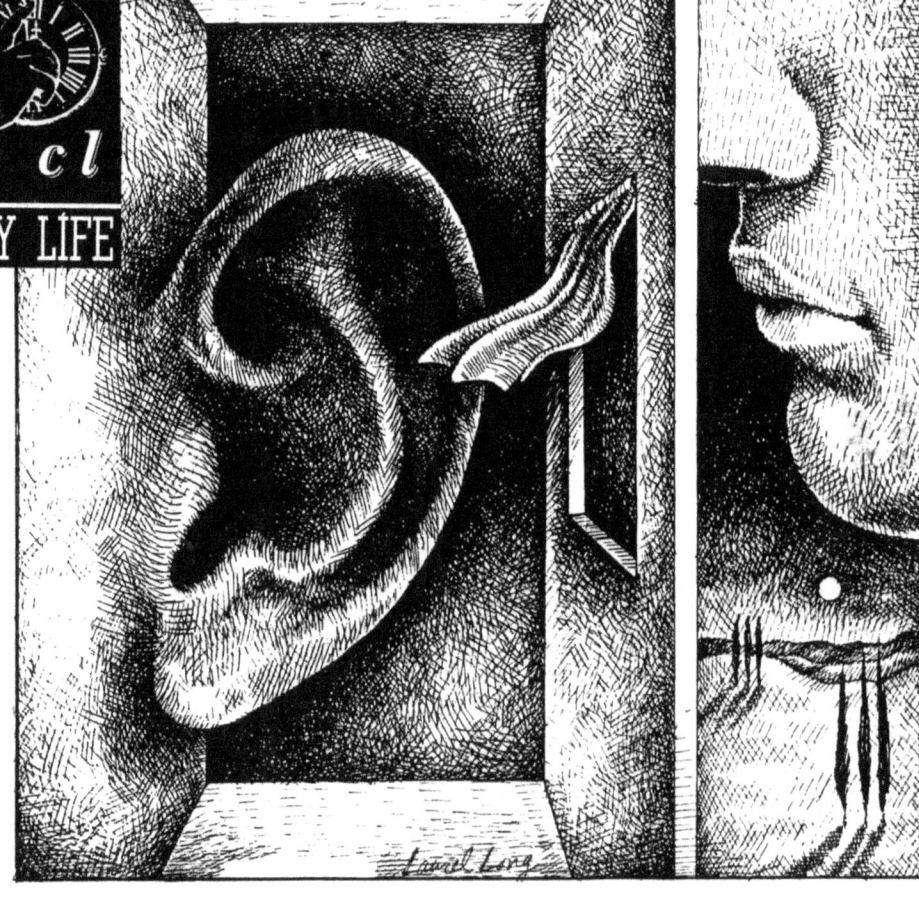

L.A. as metaphor encompasses Southern California from Barstow to Santa Monica, from Santa Barbara to Laguna, as the city's literati shape the bardic terrain. L.A. poets don't make goo-gobs of money and get considerably less respect. Yet these negatives haven't stopped the current explosion of poetry readings and workshops. Blood pumps through the amorphous heart of this cultural phenomenon via the artery of freeways linking all points. Our blood is renegade, and no poetic school can claim it. The scene is transitory by nature, and there are no rules — be recluse or self-promoter; all's allowed. Yet certain poetic landmarks, like their geographical counterparts, stubbornly persist.

Best Performer-Poet, Female
Formerly with the USO, statuesque singer-writer Linda Albertano recently toured with Alice Cooper. On stage she rivets with her astute observations of life on the edge.

Inaugurating Its Fall 1982 Reading/Performance Series
The Beyond Baroque Literary/Arts Center presents:

Performer/Composer
LINDA ALBERTANO

Linda Albertano, one of the stars and creators of the recent hit theater-performance work, SWAYBACK, and a writer/composer/performer whose exotic, amusing and chilling work has been showcased at Club Lingerie and Hop Singh's, among many other clubs and venues, will perform her songs and writings.

Plus, from New York
"Rap Poet"
BOB HOLMAN

Bob Holman is a poet/performer from New York City whose unique poetry, often based on the structures and rhythms of "Rap" songs, will be showcased in his first Los Angeles appearance. He is a director of the St. Marks Poetry Project in Manhattan and has published two books.

Friday, September 10, 8 pm
Admission: $2.00

BEYOND BAROQUE CENTER
681 Venice Blvd.
Venice, CA 90291
(213) 822-3006

SPANISH is the LOVING TONGUE

a J. Albertano

tember 24 8pm

89.9 fm

bel Holt's

omes Eclectic

Geoff Sykes

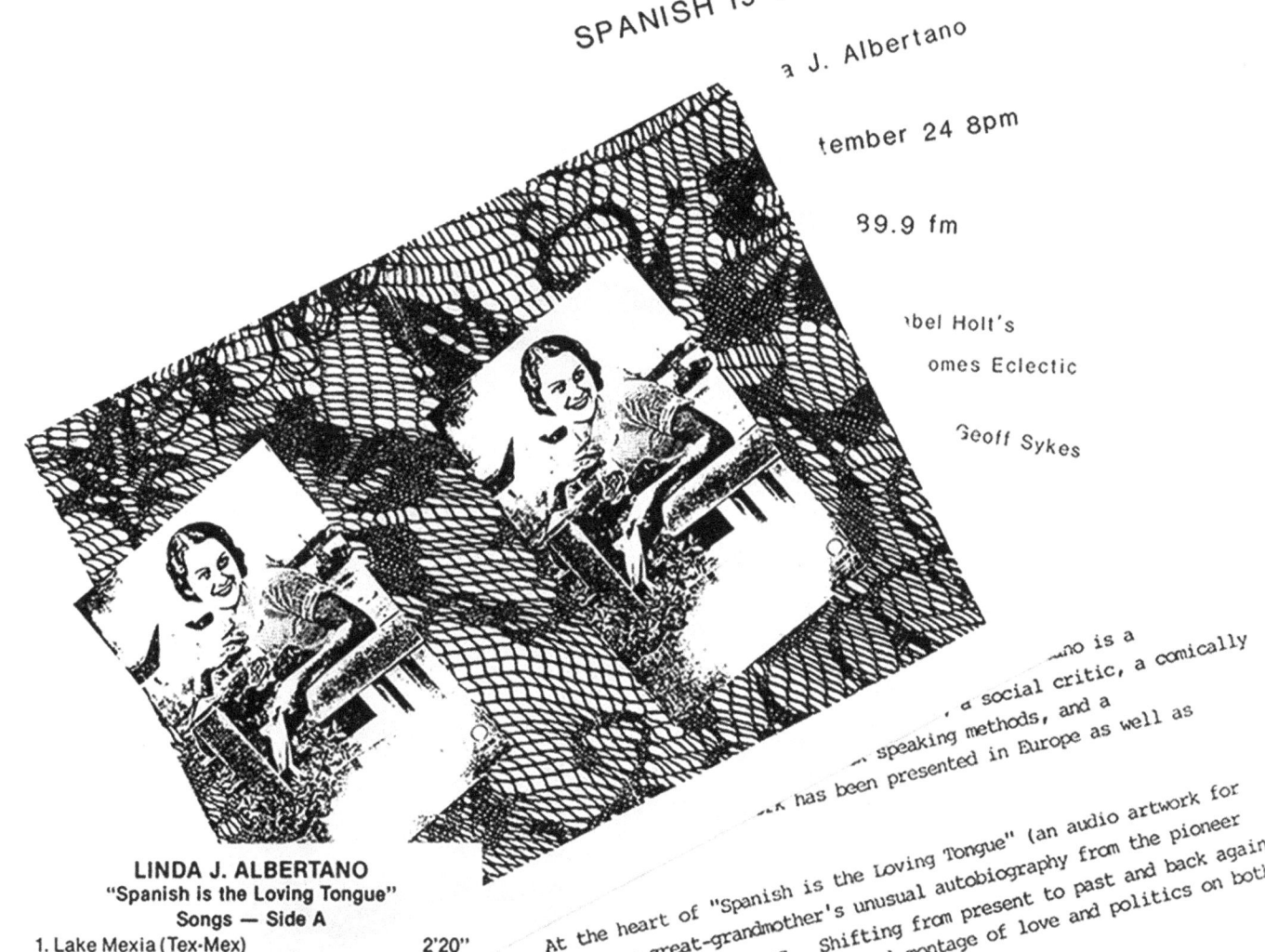

no is a
 social critic, a comically
speaking methods, and a
has been presented in Europe as well as

At the heart of "Spanish is the Loving Tongue" (an audio artwork for radio) is her great-grandmother's unusual autobiography from the pioneer settlement in Ciudad Juarez. Shifting from present to past and back again, Albertano creates a peculiar personal montage of love and politics on both sides of the border.

music by Mike McClellan

Charles Duncan

& Linda Albertano

LINDA J. ALBERTANO
"Spanish is the Loving Tongue"
Songs — Side A

1. Lake Mexia (Tex-Mex)   2'20''
lyrics: Lin Hixson; music and vocals: L.J. Albertano; guitar, vijuela, fiddle: Mike McClellan; Mad Dog Studio.
2. Lake Mexia (Gregorian)   1'13''
lyrics: Lin Hixson; vocals: L.J. Albertano; Mad Dog Studio.
3. No Holds Barred   2'45''
by L.J. Albertano; guitar, drumatix, and vocals: L.J. Albertano; drumulator: Ethan James; Radio Tokyo
4. All Night Long   5'10''
by L.J. Albertano; casio and vocals: L.J. Albertano; Radio Tokyo

Songs — Side B

1. La Malaguena   1'20''
by Ramirez & Galindo; vocals: L.J. Albertano; Radio Tokyo
2. Para Felipe   1'22''
by L.J. Albertano; translation and male vocal: Carlos Hagen; Radio Tokyo
3. Angelita Mia   3'34''
by Linda J. Albertano; drums: Kyle C. Kyle; guitar: Charles Duncan; vocals: L.J. Albertano; Mad Dog Studio.
4. Senorita Bambina   2'31''
by L.J. Albertano; casio and vocals: L.J. Albertano; drumulator: Ethan James; Radio Tokyo

All material (except La Malaguena) © & ℗ Linda J. Albertano. Cassette engineered and mastered by Geoff Sykes at KCRW, Santa Monica, CA for Isabel Holt. Introduced by Joe Frank. Tape duplicated at Studio 52 by Kris Solem, Distributed by Hermana Grande, 11 Wavecrest Ave., Suite 205, Venice, CA 90291

N²³ and THE HOUSE present

SwayBack

A Collaborative Performance Work
Written, Staged, and Performed by

LINDA ALBERTANO / MOLLY CLEATOR
JANE DIBBELL / VALERIE FARIS /
ANITA FRANKEL / LIN HIXSON /
MARTIN KERSELS / TOBI REDLICH /
MARY REID / DAVID ROSS /
ELISHA SHAPIRO / STEVE SHRIVER

Music Composed by –
LINDA ALBERTANO /
MICHAEL MONTLEONE

Produced and Directed by
LIN HIXSON

March 25, 26, 27, 28, 1982   8:30 P.M.
THE HOUSE   1329B 5th St.   Santa Monica
Reservations: 937-8779 (enter through alley)
Admission: $5

UCLA Arts Day 2006

Young Hall, Classroom 2200   Westwood, CA

May 13th, Saturday, 1:15 – 2:00 pm

See LA's most brazen
Self-Proclaimed Legends

NEARLY FATAL WOMEN

Linda J. Albertano
Laurel Ann Bogen
Suzanne Lummis

Too Cool to be Hot!
Too Edgy to be Smooth!
Too Late to be Young!

Performance followed by audience Q & A
Free admission

Sponsored by UCLA Extension Arts Department

Photo: Aldo Mauro

Blond Visitor Earns Gawks

By PHYLLIS NIBLING
Denver Post Staff Writer

A "GODDESS" descended to Denver Monday and startled quite a few mere mortals along 16th St. The 6-foot-4-inch goddess, her blond hair piled into a towering Psyche knot by the fashion oracle, Mr. Kenneth, wore a white chiffon Grecian gown.

Her chaperone, Lorraine Wilkins of New York City, who is with the John Scott Fones, Inc. public relations agency, seemed a bit vague on who she was.

"She's the Goddess," Miss Wilkins said. "She's from Mt. Olympus."

Goddess of what? Miss Wilkins kept mumuring something about soap. It seems she represents the Colgate-Palmolive account. And it seems Colgate-Palmolive manufactures something called Goddess soap.

If Miss Wilkins was after publicity, which seemed like the general idea, her goddess certainly created a satisfactory sensation in downtown traffic.

Reaction ranged from gunned motorcycle motors, wolf whistles and gawks to one little old lady's muttered "What you can see when you haven't got a gun."

"What's she doing?" one teen-ager asked Miss Wilkins. She went through her "visiting Denver from Mt. Olympus" routine.

"Where's that?" asked the teen-ager.

"In Greece."

"What is she?" he asked.

"A goddess," Miss Wilkins replied.

"See, I told you," the teen-ager told his buddy.

ALTHOUGH she was friendly enough, the goddess didn't do much communicating with the press, because "she only speaks a few words of ancient Greek," Miss Wilkins explained.

Somehow, her accent sounded more like Mt. Evans than Mt. Olympus.

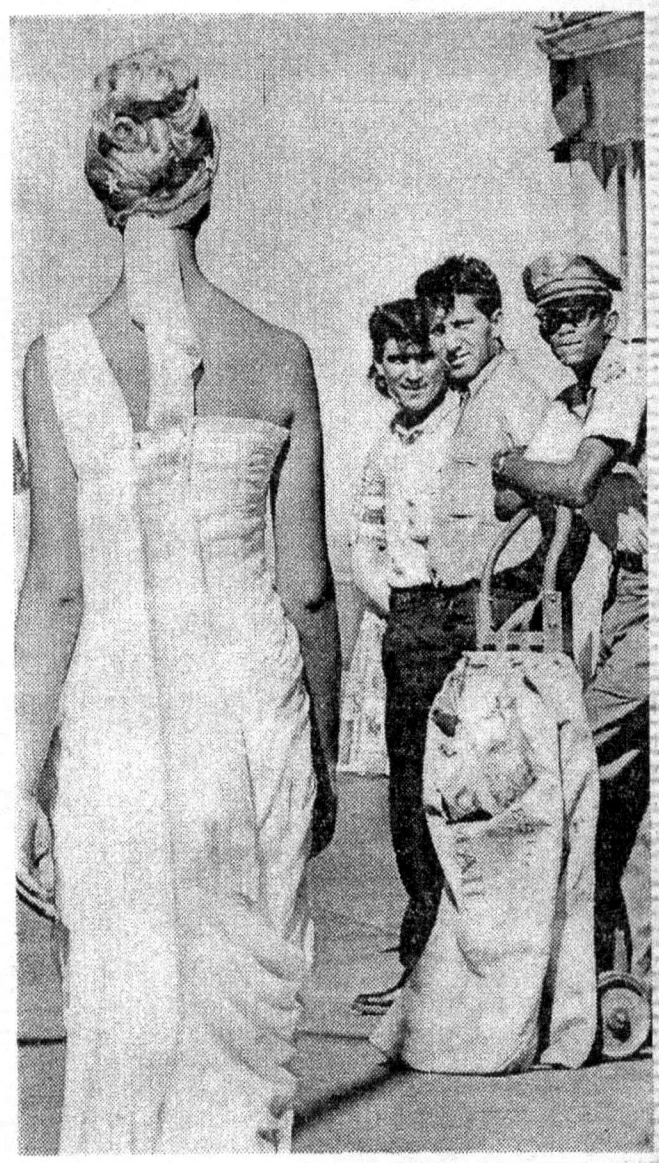

U.S. MALES LIKED WHAT THEY SAW
The blond "goddess" is 6 feet, 4 inches tall.

IT'S NOT OFTEN ORDINARY MORTALS GET A CLOSE LOOK AT A GRECIAN "GODDESS"
Junoesque visitor "from Mount Olympus" drew stares from shoppers in publicity stroll down 16th St.

Denver Post Photos by Lowell Georgia

ARTWEEK

IT'S ALIVE—ONSTAGE

Hollywood / Moe Meyer

Cabaret performance art is entertaining? Rarely. Cabaret performance art is art? Potentially. The problem lies with visual artists who approach a club stage as if it were a gallery. The variety stage format, subject to its own peculiar esthetic, remains unexplored and usually ignored altogether. The result is that all-too-familiar combination of frenzied stage action and snoozing audience.

Recognizing the presence of the audience, letting the energies of that audience alter the pacing of the performance and allowing the feedback to guide the nuances of delivery are skills too demanding for many of the cabaret performance artists. The challenge is met by seeking escape in rigidity (codified performance) and in an overall attempt to turn the piece into an art object that can then be dealt with in a more comfortable manner. When that happens, the artist loses the audience and eventually loses the art, as well.

In rare circumstances, you may catch a performance artist just beginning to discover the laws of the stage, putting a newfound awareness to work, creating a piece that is fresh and alive. Such is the case with Linda Albertano's *Pointed Sweethearts and Mercenary Children*, performed recently at the Lhasa club.

Albertano's timing isn't perfect, but she possesses a sensitive awareness of the need for it. Her institution of a sharply defined, episodic structure punctuated by blackouts takes over when personal skills

Linda Albertano (center), surrounded by children in a performance of *Mercenary Children*. Children were absent from the performance of *Pointed Sweethearts and Mercenary Children* at the Lhasa club, Hollywood.

fail her. By varying the formal design of each segment, she supplies a rudimentary, though extremely efficient, pacing that functions on automatic.

The piece opened with a Tokyo Rose-type voice broadcasting through the darkness, attempting to confuse the audience and giving a sense of things being amiss. As the six-foot-four-inch artist mounted the stage, her first monolog emphasized this feeling in a personal way. Addressing the audience, Albertano spoke of her fears of failing as a performer. This was humorously accentuated as the tape

to which she was lip-synching gradually sped out of control.

"Mr. Teenage Los Angeles," a monolog executed while Albertano lifted weights, spoke of the feeling of being a mutant at Gold's Gym, and her electronically voice-altered rendition of "Summertime" was carried out with purposely clumsy geometric poses. A clever piece communicated via semaphore described the tortures of the classic love triangle.

Two highlights, saved for the end of the piece, showcased Albertano's entertaining diversity. "Eligible Bachelors," a song in

the old GTO's style, was performed as a sleazy tab-show routine, complete with mismatched chorus boys complaining of the joys of single life. Her closing song, "Mercenary Children," was an impressive minimalist creation which left the audience wishing that she would sing more during her pieces.

Albertano has an unusually sophisticated stage sense for a performance artist working in the cabaret genre. Without having to rely on excessive use of props, shocking imagery or exaggerated movements, she has learned to place her trust in a well-designed theatrical structure. Revealing herself personally on an empty stage allows her to enter into the special relationship with the audience that this type of work needs in order to be successful.

Even though I appreciate the risks she takes by working on a bare stage, however, there seem to be many instances where Albertano panics and falls into the delivery styles of established media personae. To name only a few, I have seen her imitate Phyllis Diller, Laurie Anderson and Bette Midler—even Irma Bombeck at one point. This doesn't detract from her performance, though. It only points to her growing awareness of the need for stylized delivery, and in this knowledge she has already surpassed her local peers. □

Moe Meyer is a performance artist and a writer on the staff of High Performance.

READER

Friday, January 29, 1982 Vol. 4, No. 14 LOS ANGELES FREE WEEKLY

photograph by Steve Fine

Critic's Choice ☑

While performance artists like Laurie Anderson and Johanna Went explore music as a means of enhancing their artistic concepts, traditional singer/songwriter **Linda Albertano** heads for a similar location from the oppostie direction. Utilizing her formal musical training, Albertano combines a deceptively experimental approach with a dramatically irreverent attitude. She warps the otherwise straitlaced elements of folk to suit her adventurous musical ideas. While most of her material centers on politics, current events, and the dreaded notion of love, the means with which she communicates them vary throughout her set. Instead of sticking to guitar and piano, she often turns to her Casio (a small, hand-held keyboard/drum machine), finger-popping recitation, or simply sings a cappella in her full-throated bluesy style. Though quieter and more literal than her counterparts in performance art, the result is as witty and personal. Albertano is still new at this game, but it's exciting to wonder where she'll veer off to next. She performs Saturday at At My Place, 1026 Wilshire Blvd., Santa Monica. For free. —**Margy Rochlin**

Friday, June 18, 1982 Vol. 4, No. 34

✓ Critic's Choice

Two of the most refreshing and delightful programs I've seen this year are being put on in Santa Monica in out-of-the-way venues. Each is a unique group collaboration that dazzles the senses and resists easy synopsis, wallowing in risk taking that defies much conventional theatrical wisdom. **Sway Back** combines music, dance, humor, a slide show, and social commentary in a tightly rehearsed piece by a dozen performer/contributors, directed by Lin Hixson with music by Linda Albertano and Michael Montleone. **Outside Help** gathers together seven veterans of local improvisational companies who are letting us in on the unrehearsed process of composing a new piece about mutual epiphanies; they work under Dale Eunson's direction, frequently using marvelous props and sound instruments invented by painter/sculptor/performance artist Tom Jenkins. Sway Back may be seen for two more Wednesdays at 8 p.m. at The House, 1329-B Fifth St. (behind Palmetto). Info: 937-8779. Outside Help runs for three more Fridays and Saturdays at 8:30 p.m. at the Church in Ocean Park, 235 Hill St. Info: 399-1631. Remember, both are in Santa Monica, and are not to be missed. —**Bruce Bebb**

Friday, June 25, 1982 Vol. 4, No. 35

Sound Mix expand...

...sic coverage on page 23.

✓ **Sway Back.** This is a tightly rehearsed collaborative piece that combines dance, movement, slides, something approaching stand-up comedy, something else again that implies social commentary, and impressive music by Linda Albertano and Michael Montleone. It was written, staged, and is performed by Albertano, Molly Cleator, Jane Dibbell, Valerie Faris, Anita Frankel, Lin Hixson (who also directed), Martin Kersels, Tobi Redlich, Mary Reid, David Ross, Elisha Shapiro, and Steve Shriver. Parts of it are quite funny, and parts have the beauty and mystery of pagan rituals. In many ways this is the most exquisite show I've seen this year. (BB) The House, 1329-B Fifth St. (behind Palmetto), Santa Monica, 937-8779. Wednesday at 8:30 p.m. Closes Wednesday.

Pointed Sweethearts and Mercenary Babies. Local performance artist and musician (Sway Back, The Unseen Hand) Linda Albertano notifies us of the nature of her next presentation with the following: "is it rock & roll no is it theater no is it art no is it quantum mechanics no is it canned chicken no is it ..." My bet is that the show includes a bit of them all. Also scheduled on the same program are readings by Scott Giantvalley, Robert Tejada, and Lee Donaldson. (BB) Pilot II Theatre, 6600 Santa Monica Blvd. (entrance on Seward St.), 469-6600. Monday at 8 p.m.

SANTA MONICA Bay News

ART MATTERS

JULY 7-21, VOL. 4, NO. 1

FREE BI-WEEKLY

The Tall One, Linda Albertano

California Salad

By Claudia Lasky

Linda J. Albertano is at it again. The 6'4" poet, chanteuse and luminary performance artist is adding the finishing touches to her new piece, *Calisaladia*.. But you won't be seeing her smart-talking cabaret style performance at any of the usual art clubs, museums, or galleries she's been known to appear in.This time around, she's putting it out there for all to see, under the sky and sun, on the beach in Santa Monica

Calisaladia is a "new mini-history of the state of California," a piece that Albertano says she has been working on for the last year. It is culled primarily from casual dinner conversations that she has had at the home of her friends, Robin Love and political cartoonist Ron Cobb. She also takes as inspiration a speech she heard on KPFK given by civil rights attorney Daniel Sheehan which addressed "spiritual democracy," and contained a statement that the family is ultimately perfectible. Albertano has married the topics of history and family with fact and anecdote to convey a sense of the multicultural tossed salad that we live in, this place called California.

Albertano was a songwriter, and "I still think of things in terms of songs," she says. "My pieces are all around three minutes, and my script is the titles of the songs. When I get about a dozen of them together, it's a concert."

Albertano won't be working alone on this concert, as she usually does. "When I'm put in a big space, I feel puny. In the past, I've used slide projections to fill the space, but you can't do that outside on the beach." So she has enlisted a cross-cultural band of talented performers to fill the vast space. The cast includes poets Keith Antar Mason and Michelle T. Clinton; Native American performer Harrison Lowe; composer John Rainer,Jr; performers from downtown L.A.'s East Wind Youth Foundation; L.A. Karate Women, a school of martial artists; Chicagoans Louanne Ponder, Michael Grigo, and Ron Zisooks; and musician Eric Westfall.

Albertano will toss this crazy salad July 15, on performance platforms located where the Promenade meets the sand, Ocean Park Blvd. at Barnard Way. The action starts at 3 p.m with "The Shrimps," a performance collective going on first. The afternoon of performance is brought to you by The Santa Monica Arts Council in conjunction with The Cactus Foundation, a Performance Arts Touring/Distribution Program.

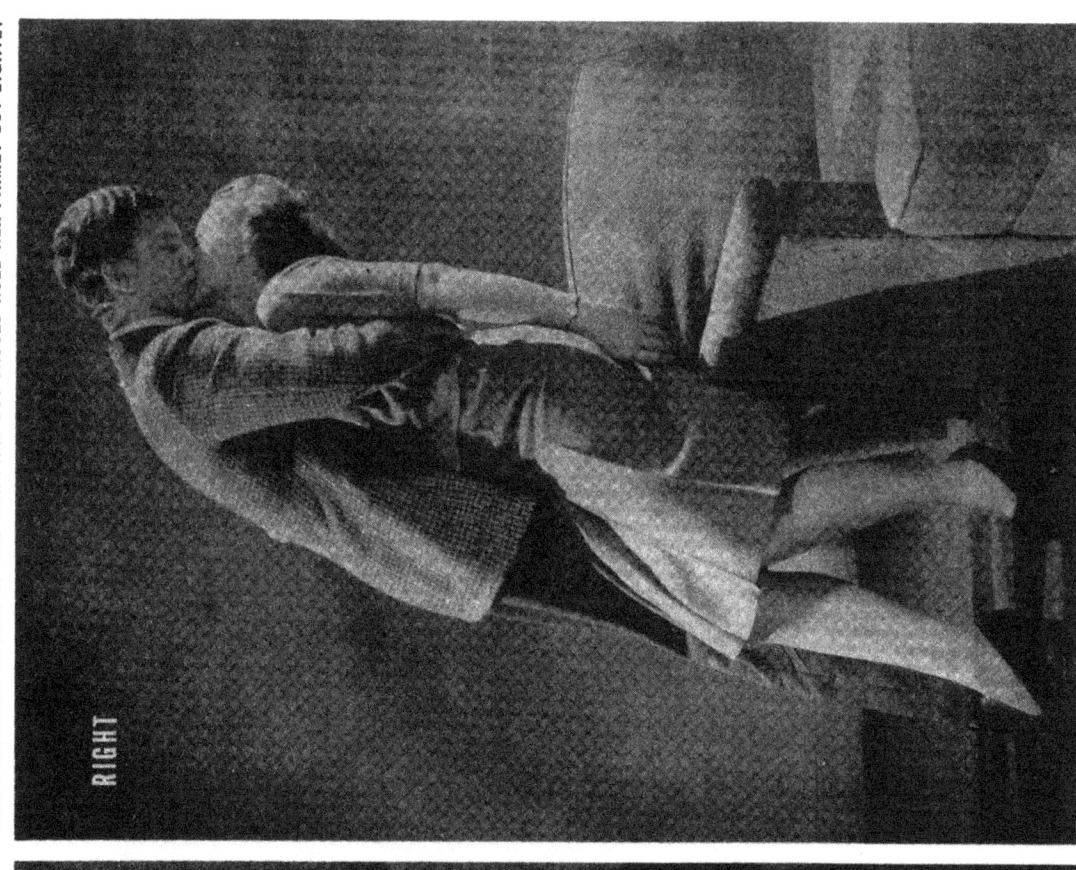

GIRL SHOULD SIT ON ARM OF THE CHAIR AND BOY SHOULD HOLD HER FIRMLY BUT LIGHTLY

RIGHT

SPRAWLING ALL OVER THE CHAIR IS CONSIDERED UNGRACEFUL. BAD TECHNIQUE

WRONG

DRUGS, POLITICS, and MODERN SEX
LINDA J. ALBERTANO AT THE LHASA CLUB
FRIDAY JAN. 27 and FRIDAY FEB. 3   10:15 PM   1110 N. HUDSON

VOICES

A QUESTIONNAIRE ASSEMBLED BY TERRY DORN

DAVID TRINIDAD

TERRY DORN

TIM'S STOLEN SWEATER
by David Trinidad

Sunlight which seeps through a part in the drapes illuminates the rumpled contents of your suitcase: sweaters and slacks, and some of those short-sleeved alligator shirts, the kind that "clones" wear, though they'd make you look good—healthy and athletic—like most of the men at the crowded bar where we met. Before we spoke, I wanted to reach across and touch your cheekbone, the scar just under the left one (I couldn't bring myself to ask how you'd gotten it, so I imagined a gang fight in your youth or a steak knife in the hand of a lover insane with jealousy). You introduced yourself. I extended my hand. Then, in your room, our chit-chat continued until, abruptly, you asked, "Do you want to kiss me?" It was a perfect way to get to the point and I was impressed. "Yes." Our movements cast shadows on flesh barely lit by the glow of the motel's neon sign as it flashed on and off. Just a few hours sleep. Now, slightly hung over, I erase one or two of the creases our bodies made in sheets a maid will change later in the day, after we've showered and dressed, gone our separate ways. You're going out for a newspaper and a six-pack. I watch you rummage through your suitcase, pull on a pair of boxer shorts, jeans, and the sweater you wore last night—light blue with thin white stripes around the chest—which is what I noticed first, from across the bar, and then, as I moved closer, how handsome you were, despite your scar.

© 1984 David Trinidad

A few months ago, Terry Dorn (the poetry coordinator for L.A.'s Anti-club and a poet himself) sent a questionnaire to a group of writers who contribute to Harvey Kubernik's spoken-word albums and related club apearances. Many of them are familiar names because of their associations, past or present, with nationally-known bands—Exene Cervenka (X, Knitters), Henry Rollins (Black Flag), Chris D (Flesh Eaters), Dave Alvin (Blasters, Knitters), John Callahan (Age of Consent) and Dennis Dragon (Surf Punks). Others, especially Linda Albertano, are known for their live "performance art" pieces. Others simply write and prefer it that way. What follows are some of our favorite answers to Terry's questions about life in Los Angeles.

1. What are the first five things that come to mind when you think of L.A.?

LINDA ALBERTANO: Palm trees; driving; loneliness; food; weather.

DAVE ALVIN: KRLA; cement riverbeds; the Lummis House in Highland Park; the orange groves I played in when I was a kid (destroyed for condominiums and houses).

JOHN CALLAHAN: Film; music; ethnic diversity; fascist police; closets.

EXENE CERVENKA: Hollywood Boulevard; live music; Harvey Kubernik; "I've Got the World Up My Ass" by the Circle Jerks; gettin' sick.

WANDA COLEMAN: October sunsets; the Lobby Inn on 120th and Avalon; Tommy's chiliburgers vs. Pink's; Motel Row (on Figueroa—I actually counted all of 'em once); low riders (as they were in the Fifties).

CHRIS D: Chorizo; cars; movie/music business (i.e. hucksters, jive turkeys); home (my friends); a living hell that seduces me to stay because it's the center of many activities I wanna do (music, film).

DENNIS DRAGON: Smog; action; film/music industries; unpredictable weather; home.

MICHAEL C. FORD: Wintertime drive-in movies has gotta be one, right? SUBURBS —all that schizophrenic geography! & i think of all the gone, violated, sunburned, corporation-burned, neglected landmarks—the mindless destruction of some of those wonderful, whacked-out fragments of architecture —not just the spikey dome on top of the academy moviehouse rickety wrought-iron cone & the mile-high cone at curry's on lake av in pasadena or the giant cement doughnut in santa fe springs, but i think of wrigley field & gilmore field smacked into splinters & pebbles. when the brooks became the l.a. dodgers, when the los angeles angels moved to spokane & the hollywood stars became the saltlakecity bees... must be five in there somewhere & gee i din get a chance to say: moviestars & the beach—too bad & they are.

KARI KROME: Cruising; Mexican food; vato graffiti; freeway murals; smog.

HENRY ROLLINS: Pollution; gross; highways; white trash; lifestylers.

IVAN E. ROTH: Dora's shrine to Elvis; the Hollywood Bowl where I saw the Beatles in 1965; the view of some row of palm trees from the Santa Monica freeway going east near the intersection of the 405 freeway; the Pantry downtown (buckwheat pancakes); aerial view of the city when you come in from the north during sunlight hours; smog shroud broken through.

2. Does L.A. have a voice or identity? Who best represents (or speaks for) L.A.?

LINDA ALBERTANO: Hunger. People want stuff. Whether it's mere food and shelter, or pink DeSotos, or billboards on Sunset. But the voice that's the loudest is the one that speaks everywhere. It's young, it's white, and it has money. I think Los Angeles magazine has its finger on the strongest pulse. It covers everything from stylish Beverly Hills murders to grisly eligible bachelors. Or dating-game type TV shows. The truest barometer of L.A.'s consumer mentality. Also representative are new talk shows in which hosts are bored by their guests and seem to be looking past them as though someone more entertaining might suddenly appear just beyond their left shoulders.

JOHN CALLAHAN: L.A. has many voices, best

represented by Harvey Kubernik's albums.

KARI KRONE: That's like asking which animal in the zoo can make the most noise.

HENRY ROLLINS: Voice? I don't think L.A. has one of its own, it's the people outside of L.A. that throw the tags on. The residents are too swallowed up.

IVAN E. ROTH: L.A.'s voice is the laugh track of television shows, the phony laughter of old voices while millions strive for some kind of recognition within the "industry."

3. Is L.A. more than a vast cultural wasteland?

DAVE ALVIN: Sure it's more. The whole East Coast concept of culture doesn't fit into folk cultures, and L.A. is becoming a home for Third World folk cultures. I'd rather have a good Mexican dinner than a subscription to *Metropolitan Museum of Art Newsletter*.

EXENE CERVENKA: Yes, it's a vast cultural wasteland with a few good people in it.

WANDA COLEMAN: L.A. is the future...More and more the nation is tilting toward the west. However, Ronnie Baby may short-stop that trend.

CHRIS D: Depends under what rock you look.

MICHAEL C. FORD: Rather it be a vast wasteland than a narrow cultural cesspool like San Francisco or New York...

HENRY ROLLINS: I think that L.A. is a total wasteland.

4. Do you like the freeways?

LINDA ALBERTANO: I hate to drive—only because the body count is high. But I have to confess a sneaking admiration for the spectacular lines of the freeway—the curved overpasses, solidly rooted columns, sweep of lights at night. It almost makes a person believe in God.

DAVE ALVIN: Yes.

JOHN CALLAHAN: Only when the traffic moves.

EXENE CERVENKA: Highway 5. North.

WANDA COLEMAN: I have a freeway jones. I know them better than I do my body. I like to drive them early in the morning to relieve tension. Beats Librium.

CHRIS D: If my car's the only one on 'em.

MICHAEL C. FORD: For me the freeway is the tangled concrete tightrope straddled by emotional acrobats trapped out there between their psyches and their central nervous systems.

KARI KROME: Yes, especially when we're driving along and my girlfriend takes off her panties and throws them out the window.

HENRY ROLLINS: Huh?

5. Do you read? If so, what?

LINDA ALBERTANO: I'm afraid I have only one vice. Magazines. I read 'em all right. All kinds...*The National Enquirer* is a must. How about those teenaged twins who won't speak to adults, are published authoresses, and are master arsonists in their spare time? You can't find stories like that in the *Wall Street Journal*—which I also like to read for the *real* news...Then there are the biker magazines, Mexican wrestling magazines, and a new one I just got—*Fangoria*—the magazine of grotesque horror movies. Nor do I neglect women's magazines—probably the best and cheapest practical advice on managing your emotions the world ever known...

EXENE CERVENKA: No, I like people to read to me.

CHRIS D: Flannery O'Connor, James Cain, Harry Crews, Cornell Woolrich, Poe, Baudelaire, Artaud, Jim Thompson, Keats, my own stuff, Iceberg Slim, William Faulkner, Mickey spillane, *Fangoria* magazine, *Psychotronic Encyclopedia of Film*, Ambrose Bierce, Thomas Hardy, Phillip K. Dick.

DENNIS DRAGON: *Popular Science* magazine.

MICHAEL C. FORD: This is where I'm supposed to say I read John Ashbury and Donald Justice and Jascha Kessler and all the fashionable heroes of modern literature. The truth is I've tried to read these guys, but the pages just start going out of focus. I don't read them bright boys with the university trained parts in their hair. They don't read me!

KARI KROME: I read a lot of periodicals. I like the instant information—why research a subject when you can have a reporter do half the work for you? Some current authors I like: J.G. Ballard, Bukowski, Iceberg Slim, *Deep Blues* by Robert Palmer, ghost stories, tall tales, folk legends, *S.T.H.* ("The Manhattan Review of Unnatural Acts"), anything on tattooing, car and bike cults, youth clubs, true crime, abnormal behavior studies, old rock and roll, anything by Richard Price for *Rolling Stone*. Anything illegal, dangerous and pagan.

6. Is the English language dead?

LINDA ALBERTANO: I don't know too much about the plight of the English language, though I suspect I'm having a limited vocabulary myself. One thing I *have* noticed is a definite dependence on the use of those fucking little four-letter words!

DAVE ALVIN: No, it changes and grows every day.

JOHN CALLAHAN: No it's evolving.

EXENE CERVENKA: I didn't even know it was sick.

WANDA COLEMAN: No, it is only undergoing metamorphosis—as usual.

CHRIS D: Not until they start giving "How to Make Rock Video" classes in schools.

MICHAEL C. FORD: Middle Latin is a dead language.

KARI KROME: No, but I think writing is becoming more clipped and economical. There seems to be less attention to detail. There's more information but less describing taste, smell, touch, sound and vision. I'd like to see a meeting of the two, a balance of the old and new.

IVAN E. ROTH: The English language is currently undergoing bypass surgery...A great renaissance of words will occur shortly. There are too many new ideas for this not to happen.

7. Do you agree with Jim Morrison when he said "The West is the best"?

DAVE ALVIN: Yeah, but the South is all right.

JOHN CALLAHAN: Yes. L.A. is the only U.S. city which ethnically reflects the world—a white minority environment which will have a tremendous positive cultural effect.

EXENE CERVENKA: He just said that 'cause it rhymes. I think he meant it at the time. I like the Santa Ana winds and that song "Mariah." I like mountain ranges.

WANDA COLEMAN: Amen.

CHRIS D: Only because you don't have to wear as many clothes as back East. But I hate all the cars and how spread out everything is.

MICHAEL C. FORD: No. I don't think Jim necessarily meant anything jingoistic by that line, it just happened to be where he was when the lyrics to "The End" were written...He'd turn geography into simply another incantation. We talked about it once in 1969, when he was looking at my manuscripts for *Sheet Music*. I remember telling Morrison that I thought location could very easily become a benediction, that people just don't know how to bless themselves with where they live. And he agreed.

HENRY ROLLINS: Don't talk to me about Jim Morrison.

IVAN E. ROTH: This is paradise.

8. Do you have any future plans?

LINDA ALBERTANO: More of the same. Life has been relentlessly swell—although it would be lovely to have a clone for the dirty work. Or better yet, a "wife" to shop, cook, and clean, do laundry, feather the nest, lick stamps, be understanding, and create a charming ambiance in which to fulfill one's ambitions. Aside from that, to be *Time* magazine's "Man of the Year" in 1987 seems a worthy goal. And that simple billboard rising above Sunset (of which I spoke earlier) might be gratifying too.

DAVE ALVIN: Keep playing guitar, writing songs and poetry. A good question would have been "Do you plan to die here?"

JOHN CALLAHAN: Yes, to direct and produce new L.A. playwrights series.

EXENE CERVENKA: Yes, everything is gonna be great, I'm gonna be happy, live a long time, accomplish a lot and have a shitload of fun with my friends and I'm gonna live to love and love to live.

WANDA COLEMAN: Sort of. But it's not wise to make plans in this man's cow town. One has to be as ready as one can be for anything any time any moment. One nevers knows.

CHRIS D: To try to be happy but I think the effort may be futile. Make more records, write screenplays, act and direct films.

DENNIS DUCK: Getting ready for "The Big One."

MICHAEL C. FORD: No.

KARI KROME: I want to travel more. I like to keep moving. It alleviates boredom, reduces bills to a minimum—and conversation is minimal out of necessity ("Do you know how to get to so-and-so" instead of "I like your pants"). People leave you alone when you're a stranger. Right now we're about to go out on the freeway again; my girlfriend just bought some new panties.

HENRY ROLLINS: I would like to open a gas chamber. I'm looking for backers and a building, about the size of the Forum. Are you interested?

IVAN E. ROTH: Yes, tomorrow I'm going to take my cousin Abbe to see the Watts Towers. I was told tonight that they are all scaffolded, but Abbe says that's OK with her because she saw the Acropolis that way.

Linda Albertano

Linda Albertano grew up with strangers, mostly in the town of Wheatridge, Colorado. Being a tall child, she was something of a teacher's pet. She always got to be hall monitor, book monitor, and window monitor. But was she popular? Possibly not.

It was in junior high, when she went on the church snipehunt, that she first realized just how different life would be for her. Darkness fell and girls started squealing like adorable piglets facing sudden, unaccountable doom. Boys, the largest of whom was 5'9", sprang to their sides, being all protective and manly. "This is absurd," she thought. She was already six feet tall in her stockings.

But there were other compensations. Raised as a Baptist, she got to sing her lungs out every Sunday.

Then, in high school, she lived in a place where there was a piano, but no metronome. Thus, she embarked on an odyssey of self-taught classical musicianship, though her sense of timing was, shall we say, quite elastic. She soon became the only youth in modern America to be forbidden to practice more than an hour a day. It sowed the bitter seeds of rebellion in her.

At UCLA she read Marx and liked it, yet it failed to destroy her drive to become a card-carrying member of the middle class. She was a filmmaking major who hung out with such arcane guys as Johnny Guitar Watson and Sugarcane Harris. They made music for her movies and inflamed her with a passion for the alltime greats...Ma Rainey, Bessie Smith, and Memphis Minnie. She emerged from college with a BFA cum laude, and a penchant for singing in sleazy Valley joints in the company of a crazed piano player and a skinny trombonist who was Kid Ory all over again.

Things took an odd turn when she fell in with real-live artists. Increasingly, she appeared in exhilarating, abstract productions like *Rest Area #17* (also known as *The Pink Piece*) and *Rockefeller Center*. She knew she was hooked when she started kicking the slats out of her own musical aesthetic and injecting what she calls "poetry, movement, and visual metaphor" into what she calls "performance".

Plunging recklessly onward, she soon began appearing in galleries, playing cheap instruments and mixing it up with originals like "Eligible Bachelors" and "Mr. Teenage California." She's also accosted audiences in clubs with such unlikely names as Hop Singh's and Club Lingerie. She did a show called *Pointed Sweethearts and Mercenary Children* at the Pilot Theatre in L.A., and was featured at both Beyond Baroque and SPARC, two centers of literary activitiy in Venice, Ca. She was a collaborator in the group performances *Swayback* and *Sinatra Meets Max*. And, assisted by Charles Duncan, she wrote and taped the music for the Cast Theatre production of Sam Shepard's *The Unseen Hand*.

Sometimes, as she works at her tiny plastic keyboard, Linda Albertano pauses; and, raising her head, she reflects on having been denied, as a child, the right to practice piano into a state of insensibility. "At last," she thinks. "This *is* the best revenge."

Then she strikes a satisfying chord and holds it until the last overtone has died.

L.A. WEEKLY

GOOD TIMES — event picks of the week

LINDA'S LAMENT

Van Halen dispatches 23 Mack tractor-trailers to haul its equipment; Laurie Anderson uses enough computer gear to safely guide Viking through the many moons of Saturn. Linda Albertano, although some inches taller than the foregoing, uses only a minuscule Casiotone to accompany her sultry moanings on the state of the sexes — moanings which, nonetheless, reveal more insight than Foreigner, more charisma than both of the sisters from Heart put together. Usually, Miss Albertano's histrionics must be experienced in drafty, small avant-garde hellholes like the Lhasa Club, Galeria Ocaso or the Anti-Club. This weekend, however, you may hear her perform her newest piece, *Wealthy Female Mudwrestling*, at a drafty, *large* avant-garde hellhole mere steps from Eagle Liquors. Opening will be Hugh Levick, self-described as a Yale-trained saxophonist-actor, for better or for worse.

—Hubert Mensch

Linda Albertano, Hugh Levick, at the Wallenboyd Theater, 301 Boyd St., dwntwn.; Fri.-Sat., Jan. 3-4, 8 p.m. Call (213) 629-2205.

Movies, Music, Art, Theater, Airwaves   January 3-9, 1986   Vol. 8, No. 6

CALENDAR

LOS ANGELES TIMES • MARCH 10, 1991 • F/W

A Poet-Performer Who Does 'Cruel Work for a Kind World'

By PENELOPE MOFFET

Linda Albertano is memorable—for her appearance (6 feet, 4 inches, with bleached blond hair and a very expressive face), for her intense performances and for the curious things she says. "Someone said poets do kind things for a cruel world," she sweetly told an Orange County audience once, "but sometimes I feel I do cruel work for a kind world."

She will present two half-hour sets about "love and limerance" at Van Go's Ear Coffee Bedlam, a tiny new cafe in Venice, on Wednesday. *Limerance,* Albertano explained in a recent interview at her Venice beach house, is psychobabble for infatuation or love addiction, a topic in which she claims some expertise. The evening will include a new piece, "The Skin of the Western World," about a love affair between an American Baptist and a Brazilian.

"I like being irreverent," Albertano said, "and in a way I think I do this kind of writing because I was never allowed to speak as a child, and at the same time I was raised as a Baptist.

"Being a Baptist has shaped me. I really intended to be a missionary. I have to temper my zeal with humor because I can be very didactic. Sometimes I really have a mission, I just want people to see things in a new light so bad."

Albertano will also participate in group readings Tuesday at Highland Grounds in Hollywood and March 20 at Van Go's Ear, and will solo March 21 at Beneath Broadway in Long Beach.

She has been drawn to the arts since she was a child growing up in Colorado. There she began teaching herself guitar and piano. Later she "sang folk songs in pizza joints," she said, while studying filmmaking at UCLA. After graduation, she had regular gigs singing with a ragtime jazz trio in what she called "Valley dives," then began appearing in friends' performance art pieces.

Albertano started presenting her own brand of cabaret performance

DAVID BUTOW / For The Times

art in 1980, and has performed at the Lhasa Club, Club Lingerie, the Los Angeles Theatre Center, Barnsdall Art Park, UCLA's Schoenberg Hall and many other venues. Her readings of her poems have also been featured on several spoken word albums from Barkubco Music (formerly Freeway Records), including the recently released "Hollyword."

Although she earned a bachelor's degree in film in 1974, Albertano didn't pursue much movie work after college. "I never wanted to work in the film factory," she said.

For a while she worked as a boom operator on American Film Institute films, but wasn't attracted by "getting up at 5 a.m. and all the coffee and doughnuts, it just didn't suit me," she said. "I'm a night person." She portrayed both a malevolent nurse and an executioner on two world tours with Alice Cooper in 1987 and 1988, and in 1988 appeared on a short-lived NBC show, "2HIP4TV." Recently she played a role as a large angel in a not-yet-released, low-budget film called "The Rapture."

She was one of three writers to work with radio producer Jacki Apple on a many-layered audio piece, "Redefining Democracy in America: Episodes in Black and White." That show, which focuses on racial politics in the United States, also featured poets Akilah Nayo Oliver and Keith Antar Mason. It premiered at Highways and aired on KPFK and other stations in February.

However, most of Albertano's work over the last year has been stripped of its more theatrical elements and special effects. These days, she usually presents her work in fairly straight readings, sometimes mixed with a few unaccompanied songs.

Economics had a lot to do with the change in her presentations, she says. Performance art "became so time-consuming, I didn't have time to earn money to live on," Albertano said. "I started to think like Michael Cimino. Once I thought of something, I had to do it. If it had occurred to me to want an elephant onstage, I'd have paid whatever was necessary. I got my mother's life savings out of her, I maxed my credit cards to the limit. I had stripped my life and my family's life bare of every resource. I had to quit, I had to go cold turkey."

Now she longs "to write about things of a personal nature, but I feel like I need bigger blocks of time. What has always happened before is that I've been seized, and just had to write something in its entirety. I think I'm suppressing that now because I have to make money."

She's working odd jobs—designing and laying tile, managing apartment buildings, selling nutritional products—to try to put her financial house in order, because "woman cannot live by poetry alone."

Her readings in Los Angeles sustain Albertano's creative spirit while she figures out how to pay the bills. With readings, she says, "you can move fast and light, you're never in debt, and you can say anything you want to say." □

Linda Albertano will perform at 9 and 10 p.m. Wednesday at Van Go's Ear Coffee Bedlam, 9 Westminster Ave., Venice, (213) 399-6870. Admission is $2. (Parking available at Speedway and Market Street.)

Moffet is a regular contributor to Calendar.

> 'I really intended to be a missionary. I have to temper my zeal with humor because I can be very didactic. Sometimes I really have a mission, I just want people to see things in a new light so bad.'
>
> Linda Albertano, *poet and cabaret performer*

Los Angeles Times

CALENDAR SUNDAY, APRIL 8, 1984

LINDA ALBERTANO STANDING TALL

By RICHARD CROMELIN

"I just feel like people aren't getting the *juice* out of life," says Linda Albertano. "I don't know why I think I should be an evangelist for getting more out of life, but I guess that's how I picture myself. Of course," she adds, "my recipe for juice is so different from other people's...."

Albertano's peculiar recipe has made the 6-foot-4 singer-poet-composer one of the few members of L.A.'s performance art community to show signs of moving beyond the rarefied gallery/museum circuit to a larger audience.

She'll debut a new work, "Spanish Is the Loving Tongue," tonight at McCabe's, on a bill of poet-musicians that includes Dave Alvin and Chuck Dukowski. She'll appear every Thursday in May at the Lhasa Club, and she plans to record her first album this month for summer release on the local Freeway/Ear Movie label. She contributed songs to Freeway's two music/spoken-word albums, "Voices of the Angels" and "English as a Second Language."

During a recent interview, Albertano remained politely evasive about her distant past, insisting that "Everything in my life happened 10 years ago—I just feel like my life started then, and there's a reluctance to talk about what happened before."

Recalling her "painful and ugly" childhood in Colorado foster homes triggered a brief flurry of tears ("So sorry... Not very adult"), and she had a ready-made quip when asked her age: "I like to think I'm a 27-year-old who's lived a hard life."

"My life didn't really get happy until about four or five years ago," she elaborated. "I'd been in therapy and it started to take." About three years ago, she discovered performance art, the experimental hybrid of various disciplines: theater, music, dance, poetry—anything that works.

"I always liked all of that stuff," she said. "If you hand me a camera I'll take pictures. If you hand me a pencil I'll draw." Albertano had been a film student at UCLA, and had sung old blues with a ragtime trio at local clubs, but when she started collaborating with performance artists like Lin Hixson and Molly Cleator, and studying with performance art guru Rachel Rosenthal, it was a new game.

"When I was singing regular songs, there was this whole convention and there were all these things you weren't supposed to do that I wanted to do.... In performance art, there was this incredible sense of freedom, it was very fun to do and people liked it.

Please Turn to Page 64

ALBERTANO STANDS TALL

Continued from 62nd Page

"I'm always at a little bit of an angle with convention. I love convention in a sense—I really like things that are popular, but I didn't want to march quite in step with everyone else."

Albertano learned about being out of step early in life. "I was 6 feet tall when I was 13," she says. "It was hell—I felt like a sideshow. I prayed for invisibility.

"It's made me a real outsider. At a very early age I realized that I couldn't be cute and cuddly and do all those things that girls are supposed to do, because it would look ridiculous. So the vision of what it is between men and women was forced upon me at a very early age.

"But it's fun now," she added. "Tall women have become more of a *thing*. There are people who will just worship me for no other reason than I'm really tall, and other people will be really put off by it—like the Boston Strangler, his favorite thing was to kill tall women. There are a lot of men who don't like their mothers."

This outsider's perspective has contributed to a brand of feminism she laughingly describes as "so hard-core that I have to keep it secret."

At a recent Lhasa Club performance titled "Pointed Sweethearts and Mercenary Children," Albertano's political passions took the form of deceptively humorous songs and poems, from a doo-wop version of "Hang on Sloopy" to a minimalist gloom-rock interpretation of "Summertime." And she skewered the upscale L.A. life style in poems like "Eligible Bachelors" and "Hey Joe": "Out here night after growling night with some female at your side/Whom you're planning on trading in as soon as her ash trays are full."

"Well, I do think that as goes L.A., so goes the world," Albertano observed. "And sometimes what's happening here isn't very pretty. It bodes ill for the human race. Of course, I get a lot of my information from reading Los Angeles magazine, and that can give you a very depressed view of life.

"It's seeing other human beings as commodities, and to me there's a horrible, terrible loneliness under it. It just breaks my heart reading these stories about men and women not being able to get together, and women saying, 'What's wrong with men?' and men saying 'What's wrong with women?' I really think that it has a lot to do with equality. I don't think that the master and the slave can be happy together.

"I think that what people really want is to be loved. But there's something about the architecture of our culture that makes that difficult."

Albertano agreed that performances like "Pointed Sweethearts" don't really convey all this political content, but she plans to remedy that: "In the next show, 'Drugs, Politics and Modern Sex,' it's a little more overt.

"But," she quickly added, "I don't want to lecture people. I still want to have fun. It should all be fun, our little trip through this vale." □

WIRE

soundcheck

Linda J Albertano
Skin
NEW ALLIANCE NAR071 CD/MC

Pleasant Gehman
Ruined
NEW ALLIANCE NAR086 CD/MC

Orchestrated spoken word recordings are the beat poetry performances for the 90s. Beat poets themselves know this: witness William S Burroughs's collaborations with both HipHoprisy and Nirvana's Kurt Cobain, as well as Allen Ginsberg's upcoming project with Sonic Youth. Now try to think of a more fertile spawning ground for spoken word than Los Angeles, that cauldron of liberalism, radical politics and punk rock. LA is the mother who spawned Henry Rollins; and here it parades two new feminist spoken word artists.

Linda J Albertano skeins surrealism and lyricism into eight fantastic pieces. The warped reality of David Lynch is an apt reference point, for Albertano's university degree is in film making; vivid images splash colour into her tales. Lush language and carefully chosen aural bites cultivate texture in a world seeping with heat and saturated with history, a world unburdened by chronology.

Sexual and political power relations form Albertano's stomping ground. With satire and simile as her tools, she unravels scenarios, attempting to uncover their subtexts. Ladykilling Casanovas are lampooned as she invites you to spend Valentine's Day with Lucifer As he reels yet another trusting victim into his trap, Albertano reminds you that no matter how charming he seems, *"There will be no bouquet for the lady"*. In "Nero At The Barbeque" we accompany the blase Roman on a tour of East LA circa the Rodney King riots. Pontius Pilate and the leader of ruling LA gang The Crips fight for turf over a game of chess: *" A homeboy in a teeshirt... moves his black knight to Pico and Fairfax/Check!/Buildings flame into the darkness as cheerfully as birthday candles/The President flips a scorecard/Points for the homies."* A commentary that entertains and educates as it inquires.

JULIE TARASKA

Barney Bush/Tony Hymas/Tony Coe/Shawnee Nation United Remnant Band Drum
Remake Of The American Dream
Volumes 1 & 2
NATO 53012/53013 CD

On 31 July, 1918 in the last days of the First World War, as an act of self-determination and moral pride, the Onondago Indian Nation declared war on Germany. In global terms it was only one of a group of late declarations by previously neutral countries eager for a seat at the conference table, but in the political history of Native Americans it represented a symbolic turning point.

70 years later, the Shawnee Nation United Remnant Band Drum set the seal on another Representing a rump of the four Shawnee bands who had refus to negotiate with the Federal Government and had thus be

Poets Reading, Inc.

II i 1990

the quarterly

LINDA ALBERTANO –
High Priestess of Power Politics

In the early '70s, poet Linda Albertano scored a victory fighting on the front lines of the feminist movement.

Linda, then a film student at UCLA, decided she wanted to become a waiter. She was working as a hostess and cocktail waitress to pay for her education. Management at the restaurant told her that only men were physically qualified to be waiters. "Of course, I'm six-foot-four, and strong as an ox," she says, "and I could beat half the guys there at arm wrestling."

Hoping to discourage her, management insisted that, according to company policy, all waiters must have been a busboy first. Linda took them at their word, and soon management was unable to deny that she had mastered the art of bussing tables.

"Rather than have me be a waiter, which would have caused a revolution, they offered me a management position," she recalls. She and another woman were among the first in the entire company to be accepted into management.

"We trained hard, and we went up to San Francisco, and we took the corporate test. The two management trainees returned to Southern California and awaited their test results. The head of the region came down shortly thereafter.

"He said that he just knew that we were going to be an embarrassment to him, and that he was going to 'ride us hard,' remembers Linda. "Of course, when the test results came back we were at the top of the class, and we were sensational managers."

Linda put her new found power to use. "I started encouraging all the young women who came there to go for the higher paying jobs, and to become waiters and cooks and bartenders," she remembers.

The resulting emasculation led to a legal dispute between the female buspeople and the company, which was settled out of court. "The moral of the story was that those middle managers who had made life so hard on us were eventually fired. Every position in that restaurant was integrated," Linda says, "and it completely broke the back of sexism in that restaurant."

In her poetry, as in her life, Linda calls for the male-dominated social hierarchy to be stood on its head, putting women on top. In GOD'S FAVORITE ANGEL, a 21 year-old prostitute brings a television evangelist to justice. "Her body is the temple of God. God wants the money changers out," Linda writes.

In THE GOLDMINER MANIFESTO, Linda envisions the day when economic power, achieved through corporate sabotage, palimony, and stealth, is controlled by women. "And the buff bodies of nubile boys draped across the hoods of sexy roadsters in magazine auto ads will make our credit cards throb with unquenchable Joy!"

THE GOLDMINER MANIFESTO is part of a radio program by Linda aired on KPFK in 1986. Linda calls it "an iconoclastic look at the world. I created a fictional character called Sugar Reynolds, who's the editor of a magazine called GOLDMINER. It's a cross between PLAYBOY and FORBES," Linda explains. The program is a visit to Reynold's mansion.

"Sugar Reynolds is addressing the imbalance of eroticism," she explains. "She is attempting to eroticize the male." How is this done? "She puts powerful men in the foldout with the symbols of their power, which are usually economic. She poses them on beds of gold bullion, and that sort of thing."

If Sugar Reynold's approach makes one do a mental double take, then Linda has succeeded. "I think that one of the purposes of art is to allow people to see things in a fresh way, which you can do by taking things apart and reassembling them," Linda explains. "If I say that I don't believe in equal wages for equal work, and that I think women should earn twice as much as men, that affects people viscerally. They suddenly see the injustice of one group of people earning twice as much as another."

There are those who feel that Linda's message is too extreme in its reversals of gender stereotypes. Traditional feminists have voiced their disapproval of her neo-feminist approach to art. "For example, if I say something about photographing the president of ITT naked on a bed of gold bullion, they might pull me aside afterwards and give me a talk about how 'we don't really want to objectify another human being, that's not the feminist creed'."

What sets Linda apart from the rest of the feminist flock is her savvy about the entertainment needs of her audience. "I'm pulling away from dealing with the issue seriously, because I'm trying to reach those people who can't be reached with serious rhetoric."

However, when seriousness is appropriate, Linda pulls no punches. In AN OPEN LETTER TO THE SCHOOLGIRLS OF AMERICA, she presents her naive charges with a grim reality, encouraging them to question their fantasies and to face the facts. The poem is a call to eliminate ignorance about rape and physical abuse of females by males. "What I'm trying to do is to inform the victim, so that they can understand that this is a phenomenon that is not their fault, that it's widespread, not to give 100 percent trust to the people that they commonly trust, like husbands, teachers, employers," Linda says. "I really wish I could send it to every schoolgirl in America."

The hope for gender equality is indeed in the hands of the younger generations. The feminist movement is no longer thriving as it was in the '70s. "It seemed that everybody felt the revolution was over. They felt that, all of a sudden, there were a lot more female doctors and cops on T.V." Linda says. "It's not a big topic of conversation among my friends that women are only making 52 cents on the dollar."

Perhaps the "movement" needs more people like Linda Albertano.

by Keith Walsh

Linda Albertano appears at L.A.C.E. (1804 Industrial St., downtown Los Angeles) exhibit January 20 & 21, 8 p.m., in the exhibit "Moving Towards the Millenium."

The Firefly

To be the light in your life
Means being kept prisoner
In a small glass jar.

by Dawn Allred-Viotto

She lit up the stages she visited with profusions of words that sparkled in the air, her mellifluous voice giving tonic beauty to each syllable of her works. She loved life and poetry and especially us, we the people. Her lines of words will motivate and melt forever the hearts of those of us who read them, and at times help us laugh with joy. She was and will remain

Linda J. Albertano, Poetry Diva.

IN MEMORIAM

PART IV

WHY I BECAME A WRITER

When I was four years old and living in Colorado, my lovely, creative, bohemian mother taught me to read and bought me a set of twelve books for Christmas ranging from "one, two, buckle my shoe" all the way to Proust and Kropotkin in the twelfth volume. Then my parents separated. My brother and I became latch-key kids who were soon captured by an almost sinister foster system where we were held hostage from grade school to the end of high school. The books went into storage and were never seen again.

Because Mom looked like a gypsy to the sour social workers who had placed us in the strictest of fundamentalist homes, we were not allowed to see her. Well, we did see her once. But when it was time to go, they had to pry us, sobbing, from her comforting arms. She was all joie de vivre, curls piled in an upsweep, glorious dangling earrings, peasant blouses, and flowering circle skirts. Her red lips and high, high heels must've made others feel stunted and misshapen. And . . . she smoked. A cardinal sin. The agency labeled her the devil and barred her from visiting.

In foster so-call "care," I learned the meaning of shame, blame, and corporal punishment. I was forbidden to speak in my own defense or for any other reason. I wore silence like a heavy sackcloth. At school I kept to myself, as no invitation to play or go to another's home could be accepted. There would be no birthday parties. Ever. Anything beautiful, interesting, or fun was deemed a sin. I lived in a cultural desert devoid of company, conversation, or gaiety. Outside of school the only book I saw was the bible.

Upon graduation, the institutional gates swung open. My adoring and adorable mother drove from her home in Montana to present me with a guitar—the perfect gift! I began to express myself like mad through songs and songwriting. My partner and I came up with a couple of tunes recorded by Linda Ronstadt (on

The Stone Poneys), Taj Mahal (on *The Rising Sons*), and Carolyn Hester, among others. Ultimately, I went to a songwriting workshop where I was informed that I "didn't fit the mold." I left, remembering Jean Cocteau's dictum, "Do what they hate. It's YOU!"

Kicking out the last slats of conformity, my offerings became a kind of art which I took up and down the coast and all over town from the Lhasa Club and other venues to the John Anson Ford and LATC, and well as to London and Edinburgh. Invited to read the text of my performances at One World Poetry Festival in Amsterdam, I was honored to receive an enthusiastic review of my poems from Harold Norse in *Poetry Flash*. It was as though I'd been freed from a grim tutelage of silence. At last! I was permitted to speak!
    And that's how I became a writer.

—**Linda J. Albertano**

The Original Nearly Fatal Women

PART IV

THE WAY WE WERE: NEARLY FATAL

Suzanne Lummis' memories of Nearly Fatal Women for Beyond Baroque's anniversary anthology, featuring tributes, memories, and responses to the question, "Why do you write?" from poets and those affected by that arts center. The publication's called The Writing Life: 55 Years at Beyond Baroque.

Too cool to be hot. Too edgy to be smooth. Too late to be young. And then there was that other promo line: Just when you thought you were safe from the adverb, nearly!

For 20 years, we were L.A.'s seriocomic, semi-shameless, eccentric, and text-centric Nearly Fatal Women—Linda Albertano, Laurel Ann Bogen, Suzanne Lummis. The late (but recent) legend in the Los Angeles performance art world, Jacki Apple wrote, "They're wonderful. They're outrageous. They're women on the edge, and over."

And we got a write-up in New York, from Peter Fortunato, professor at Cornell University: "These three women, these three poets from the City of Los Angeles, have their performance licks tuned up, their wit honed bright, and a sense of humor, a collective tone that avoids strident polemics while affirming humane values."

It all began at . . . let's see . . . Where was it? Oh yes, we debuted at Beyond Baroque Literary Arts Center in Venice. And the year was 1995. Or 1994. Neither Laurel nor I can remember for sure, and that magnificent, joyous, embodiment of much of what's good in the world, Linda Albertano, died in fall of last year, age 80, after a life filled with enough variety and adventure for four lives. Make that five. Therefore, we can't ask her. And, anyway, she probably wouldn't remember either.

In the beginning, we were four women, Anna Homler, creator, or inhabitor, of "Bread Woman," was also a Nearly Fatal in that first show, then her solo career took her overseas. In '94 (or '95), after cobbling together a selection of our poems or prop driven creations, to be performed solo or collectively with staging, objects and attitude, and after rehearsing like mad, we presented this thing we'd created in front of a good-sized audience of poets and aficionados of experimental performance. At the end, we ran off stage to our green room, AKA the women's restroom.

We stood breathless for a couple moments. Wild applause resounded from Beyond Baroque's performance space, but something else also, a thundering, a sort of pounding. I looked at Laurel, Linda, and Anna, I said, "In the theater world, that is what is known as a curtain call."

We ran back out and did some bows, or did something, and whatever we did was no doubt unsynchronized because we hadn't prepared or rehearsed for an ovation—especially not one this noisy.

Later, the fine poet Richard Garcia, of all people, one of the least demonstrative poets I knew, confided to me, "I was the one who started the foot stomping."

On June 20, 2013, another date neither Laurel nor I remembered, but Cece Peri—who staged managed for us did, we gave what would turn out to be our final performance, though by then we'd performed at The Knitting Factory in Manhattan, at Cornell University, at the university in Knoxville, Illinois, and even made it down to Southwest College, South San Diego County. We'd wound up where we started. Some in the audience said later that as often as they'd come to Beyond Baroque, they'd never seen as many people packed into that space.

In fact, before the show, the audience pouring in, our performance area shrinking as people began sitting down on the floor in front of the first row of chairs, the turn-out reached the "good problem to have stage." And I remember exactly when it crossed into the "beginning to be an alarming problem to have" stage, when Richard Modiano led yet another person through the concentrated bodies and set him down on the crowded floor. I said, "Richard! When I come out to do my Medusa as a Van Nuys biker chick, a red spot is supposed to come down on me. But it's not going to—it's going to come down on that guy sitting there! So, I hope he has something prepared." And Richard, who rarely loses his temper, snapped, "Well, what am I supposed to do?!"

He closed the door on any late arrivals then, and—wouldn't ya know—a couple of my friends got turned away.

We didn't figure that'd be our last show, but a while later we lost our sound and lighting guy—he moved out of state. And there was no other equally skilled ("sound") sound and lighting person to be had. That was part of it. Also, each of us got busy with other madcap endeavors.

So, we Nearly Fatal Women wound up where we began, just like the lines from Eliot's "Four Quartets." "We shall not cease from exploration/ And the end of all our exploring/ Will be to arrive where we started/ And know the place for the first time."

I'm not sure those lines are entirely applicable, not sure that the debut and grand finale of our performance trio was quite so suffused with transcendent meaning—but I love the sound of them.

Even after we stopped performing, among the three of us, the name endured. When together, for each other's birthdays, Christmas, and movie-going (oh, we saw so many movies); we knew who we were. The Nearly Fatal Women.

An excerpt from a poem by Suzanne that Nearly Fatal Women performed on that first night at Beyond Baroque.

> On the second night I dreamed
> I was rounding a corner and guessed
> I was about to get caught.
> There was a shape on the other side, some
> criminal set to go for his mark. I froze
> like game, but it was only you with your high
> opinion of yourself and canceled credit,
> you with a card trick in one back
> pocket, tiny cross dangling over your heart,
> an alibi on the tip of your tongue.
> It was you going after my secrets and keeping yours.
>
> It was not you I wanted but climate, Fahrenheit,
> that altitude where the air is thin but still holds heat.
> I wanted weather and the weather forecast. I wanted
> the late-breaking news.
>
> I wanted it delivered to my door. I wanted landscape,
> seascape, China and a boat to sail there, a whole
> fleet, emeralds, steamed milk and honey served to me
> on an enamel tray. I wanted to be served. . . .
>
> **—Suzanne Lummis**

Poems and Stories by

Linda J. Albertano

FAVORITE MEMORIES OF BEYOND BAROQUE

In trying to squeeze into the cultural and social shapes around me, I'd accumulated more rejection than seemed healthy or necessary. So, as I've revealed elsewhere, I decided to embrace Jean Cocteau's contrarian philosophy of art. In my first incarnation of Cocteau's credo, having tossed the conventions of songwriting into the trash bin, I managed to appear at SPARC, Venice's Social and Public Art Resource Center.

My debut there earned me a "Pick of the Week" for an upcoming event in Santa Monica. However, a few days after I'd rolled out my songs without rules, the booking agent from At My Place called to tell me that I'd been permanently banned from the club once they'd witnessed my unorthodox performance.

This news should have left me as shattered as a broken window in an abandoned, self-recriminating room. Instead, I was buoyed by internal vindication. Dennis Cooper and Benjamin Weissman had been in the audience that night and had invited me to perform with Bob Holman at Beyond Baroque! It was a last-minute cavalry rescue, just like in the movies!

That was only the first of many memorable moments. God lifting the roof of a serial killer's domicile in Dennis Cooper's vivid novel. Benjamin Weissman's wry wit and ability to wield language like a drum major's baton—twisting it, turning it, and sailing it into the air in the most unexpected ways. Scott Wannberg's lively birthday celebration mobbed, as it was, in the lobby and up the center stairs. Pam Ward's delicious laughter. The ubiquitous Doug Knott.

The stunning documentation of L.A. poets by Mark Savage and, again, by Alexis Rhone Fancher. The Poetry Wall. Pegarty Long's Philomenian. The literary and musical musings of Brad Kay and Suzy Williams. Prince Diabaté's Beyond Baroque concert, in which L.A.'s West African denizens rose from their seats to dance elegantly and shower him with paper money, as is their custom. The citywide "Noirfest" masterminded and curated by the inexhaustible

Suzanne Lummis. ANY of their own poems as read by Michael C. Ford or Laurel Ann Bogen.

Presenting one of two versions of Steve Goldman's birthday poem "Several Self-Gestapos . . . " Performing countless times with the other Nearly Fatal Women, Laurel Ann Bogen and Suzanne Lummis. Finally, being forced to turn audience away due to obscene overcrowding! Jim Fleck, the lighting and sound technician who answered the call always, and who was truly one of us.

Dada fests and Dada poets, and those who make it happen, Kat Georges and Peter Carlaftes. SA Griffin's poetic observations, modern yet timeless, human, surprising, full of heat and heart. His miraculous ability to create and hold a sacred space for the community of souls at Beyond Baroque. David Zasloff's soaring and whimsical, profound, and profane eulogy for Austin Strauss. And, of course, the vibrant incantations of Richard Modiano, filling the room with urgent reasons to support Beyond Baroque as well as the poets it hosts. And, at the same time, making us all glad, glad, glad to be a part of it!

Linda Albertano at Venice Poets' Wall

TO THE PACIFIC

To the Pacific!
Who is older than wisdom.
Who is shrinking like the slow death of thought.
Who is caught in a storm behind our ribs.
Who finds her rhythm in the delirious
      heartbeat of night.

It's dark.
Where were we when the lights went out?
Who poured the last round?
It's dark.
It gets dark in here fast.
 To the Pacific!
Who throbs in our improbable bodies.
Who breathes us in and out.
Who sings between Earth and Orion.
Who makes us feel taller than trees.
Who suffers the weight of our pain.
Who's been trained to submit to our whims.
Whom we'd bring to her knees if she had them.
Who's been trapped in a terminal brothel.
Whom we've cast in an X-rated movie
      and we're waiting to watch her bleed.

It's dark.
By the nature of our deeds we're dirty.
We're bound in our own senseless chains.
It's dark. How long can this last?
It's sad. Is it criminal? Or criminally insane?
It's dark in here.
It gets dark in here fast.

To the Pacific!
Who surprised us with the curious
invention of life.
Whose intentions were purely honorable.
Who stirred our first shimmering cells.
Who helped us crawl up on her shores.
Whose blood still roars in our ears.
Whom we've caged like a laboratory rabbit
blinded with stinging rain.
We're boys pulling wings from sparrows
    obliviously nonchalant.
We spend her like sailors on benders
    ignoring her desperate eyes.
She's kidnapped for the intangible joyride.
She's dropped in the vestigial ditch.
How quickly we tire of our toys.

It gets dark.
It gets dark in here fast.
We are pushing her past her prime.
We shout petrochemical lies!
Time sticks in our indecent throats.
It gets dark, it gets dark, it gets dark in here fast.
And where were we when the lights went out?
Where were we?

To the Pacific . . .
    to her we belong!

She holds no wrongheaded notion of justice.
She builds no concrete tomb for our lungs.
She forces us to feed on no poison.
She hangs us from no twisted tree.

She rids us of no personal medfly.
She plants no bomb in our gut.
She crushes no skull for freedom.
She nails us not to the ground.
She studies us not into extinction.
Her changes are slower than rivers.
History melts in her mouth.
She'd deliver us from evil if we'd let her.
How long have we been lost?
And where were we when the lights went out?

It's dark. It's dark.
It gets dark in here fast.

To the Pacific!
You are bluer than our insignificant eyes.
You are saltier than the tears we cried
      when we heard you might die of
our neglect.
We're killing you with exquisite indifference.
You've washed our feet with your grief.
We're gathered on the courthouse steps.
We're bargaining one more plea.
We're praying they'll spare you from us.
Our blood is screaming your name!
We're tearing up the deed to your being.
We'll love you more deeply than death.
We're prepared to pay the better price.
We'll rip the tainted needles from our veins.
Our blood is screaming, is screaming your name!

We are about to become more serious.
Where were we when the lights went out?

To the Pacific!
Older than unbearable wisdom.
Shrinking like the pointless death of thought.
Caught in the fire storm in our heads.
Tattooing the sacred skin of night.
Pounding in our hopeful bodies.
Breathing us in and out.
Shouting Hosannas under Orion!

Drench us with unquenchable life!
Your waves are breaking deep inside!
Your blood is roaring in our ears!
You are dreaming us awake!
Make us feel taller than trees!
Dance us in your pagan arms!
Your drums are beating on our shores!
We're comprehending what you'd have us do!
We're sounding louder alarms!
We long to be truer believers!
We'll be strong in our will to prevail!
And we belong, we belong, we belong to you!
It's to you that we belong!

You've made your mark on our souls.

But it's dark in here.
Don't let the lights go out.
We're about to become more serious.
Don't let the light disappear.

Don't ever
let the light

disappear.

BELOVED

Thou art incendiary.
Thou sendest me up in sparks
                100 times a day.
Thou makest me hum like 1000
       buzzing phone lines yammering through
              dizzy night.

When thou smilest upon me, I'm
       money in the bank.
When thou snarlest, I am as a bad
       check, bounced, and cowering
       in thy heart's darkest dumpster.

Thou art the Lion of La Cienega,
       the Rose of Sherman Way.
       I love to lay eyes on thee.

Thou ringest through me sudden
       and bright as fresh champagne.
My switchboard overloadeth.

Thy breath is as clean laundry
       folded behind thy lips.
Thy teeth art as white Cadillacs
       parked in neat rows.

I love to taste the texture
       of thy skin.
Thine eyes art interstellar.

Beloved,
       thou art incendiary.

Thou sendest me up in sparks!

ALL NIGHT LONG

I went to your house last night
all night long.

I was early.
It was a bad sign.

Your friend answered the door
all night long.

He said you were asleep.
It was a bad sign.

He invited me in
all night long

to talk.
It was a bad sign.

I locked myself in the closet
all night long

in the dark.
It was a bad sign.

I could hear you sleeping
all night long

through the walls.
It was a bad sign.

An engine was idling
all night long

in my chest.
It was a bad sign.

I wanted to change my clothes
all night long
but I couldn't get it right.
It was a bad sign.

Your friend talked to me
all night long

through the door
It was a bad sign.

He said "You and me, babe,"
all night long.

I said "My heart belongs to another."
It was a bad sign.

He said "Another's been steppin' out on you, Babe!
All night long.

Why not do the same?"
It was a bad sign.

"All right," I said, "All right."

Your friend is my type
all night long,

but you have more women.
It was a bad sign.

You have more.
   All night long

      You have . . .

         You.

            You.

               You.

APRÈS LA PANDÉMIE

Robots exuberantly reboot humanity right in the kiester. Merde!

Neo-technical feudalism grows like crabgrass on the moldering corpses of cafés. Non! Ce n'est pas vrai!

Our new world tastes like rotisserie rubber chicken. Ou la même chose . . .

Hope?   Or Change??   Take yer pick in the post-human universe. Mais pourquoi?

We may NOT pass GO. We may NOT collect $200. Rien pour nous!!

Our pockets are filled with fun-sized, flat-screen coliseums for maximum mind-meldage. Dors . . . mes enfants.

A Philip K. Dick replicant promises from the drum-drop, hip-hop beat of the machine behind his tin ribs to protect us and to visit us often. Comme les animaux?

Our mischievous moments, our scintillating histories, the mysteries of our echo, the contents of our shimmering dendrites and neurons will be shoveled into gaping, grey boxes in perpetuity. Quel dommage!

Après la Pandémie . . . ??
Voici! Notre bebe!!

THE REAL HOUSEWIVES OF THE RIVER STYX

So you traded your free speech for 30 pieces of silver.
You crushed your right to report real news
under an avalanche of PR for the Goblin of Greed.
Remember? *It may not be good for America,*
but it's DAMN good for CBS!

Profits before Principles. Profits of Doom.
Daddy owns the Pentagon, and that sticky black goo
that fuels your artificial ignorance is NOT
Coca-Cola, Baby, it's liquid cyanide!
Sayonara from the Death Star.

You toady up to the in-crowd and turn your scaly backs
on your WikiLeaks bro while he's lynched and dismembered!
Good thinking, media camp-followers.
Soon you'll ALL be torched with flaming Pentagon Papers.

It's your art. It's official.
It's pure, purposeful, perpetual ignorance.

AI. AI. AI.   Ay, yi, yi, yi, yi!   Artificial Ignorance.

Joke's on us.

BUSY

(Note to the Reader. Poem to be read in an increasingly rapid word speed.)

"I'm sooo busy," she said.
"I've really been terribly, terribly busy."

"You ha-ave?" remarked her friend,
"Why, what a coincidence,
I've been busy, too. I've been <u>very</u> busy.
Why I've been extremely, extraordinarily busy."

"<u>You've</u> been busy," said a <u>third</u> party,
who was simply eavesdropping on the street.
"You think <u>you've</u> been busy, let <u>me</u>
tell <u>you</u> what <u>busy</u> <u>is</u>. <u>I'm</u> busy.
I am a very busy person.
I have been sooo busy. Why, this year,
I have been busier than I have been
all other years put together.
Just in the first few months, barely.
You can't imagine how frightening it is,
not to be able to have time
to get down to the Discount
App Store. I mean, that's how
very busy I've been!"
"Oh, yeah?" said her friend, "Well,
I have been too busy to have <u>my</u>
smart phone respond to <u>your</u> insulting tweets."

"Oh, yeah?" retorted the very first to speak,
"Well, let me tell you this—I have been too
busy—even to take lunch. I get my meals through
an intravenous hook-up. Next to my desk. Where I work.
At TikTok."

"Oh, yeah? Meanwhile, I been doing
a hundred-and-twenty miles an hour
on the Poetry Superhighway.
Catch me if you can, Copper!"

"Oh, yeah?"

"Oh, yeah?? Well let me tell you
how busy I've been. I have been
frighteningly, astoundingly, shockingly
busy with my very busy
frightening, shocking, and astounding schedule!
There isn't one tiny piece of light
that can shine through any crack
in my schedule. Because I am just . . . I've, I've g . . .
I'm quintuple-booked is how busy I am.
That's how very, very busy I am."

"Because I'm, I'm such busy person,

I've just been really, really busy.
I've been, I've been busier than you can imagine."

"No one knows how busy I've been.
I've been busier than the speed of light.
I've been really, really busy."

"I mean I'm busy. I, I'm so busy.
I'm, I'm . . . Wait! . . . I don't know, I dunno how to,
how to explain how busy I am . . .

I'm really, really busy, I'm very busy.
It's . . . wait, no, HELP! No, WAIT! I'm
too busy, I'm too busy. I've been very busy.
I'm a very busy, busy person! Busy, busy, busy!
don't you understand? I mean <u>busy</u> when I say busy!
I'm not kidding, I'm serious. I mean busy! Really
busy, busy, busy!"

"Wait! Oh, Stop! Oh, Help!
Somebody help me. Somebody.
Somebody stop me. Stop me.
Someone stop me before I <u>do</u>
one more thing!"

GOD'S FAVORITE ANGEL

Jesus is on vacation. He needs the rest.
He puts in a lot of overtime. It's a new
world. He just doesn't know. Nothing seems
to work any more. He heeds the rest. Maybe He
should get a Master's in Business Administration.
He really doesn't know.

But right now, He's on vacation.

Jesus really loves reggae. They're talking to <u>him</u>,
Mon. And he looks good in dreadlocks. Jamaica
Sun Splash. Reggae 'til you drop, Mon. He
needs the rest.

God's favorite angel is sleeping. She puts in a lot of
overtime. She's on a mission. She needs the rest.
She does some of her finest work at night. She's
on a special mission. Right now, she's tired.

Her body is the temple of God. God wants the
money-changers <u>out</u>. She's on a mission. She
does her finest work at night.

Jesus is on vacation.
And God's favorite angel is asleep.

They need the rest.

God's favorite angel is dreaming. Of Emilio
Estevez. He's in a Vietnam war movie. It
seems to be raining bullets. He reminds her
of Jesus Christ. Though Christ rarely wears fatigues.
Her alarm clock goes off. It's late in the day.
Time to get ready for work. She's at her best at
night. She's on a mission.

God's favorite angel steps into a pair of panties.
Expensive. Red lacy bikinis. Mmm. With a matching
push-up bra. Yes! Plunging bustline. Mmm. Hook in front.
Yes! She fixes her fish-net stockings. Mmm. She squirms into
a small satin dress. She looks so hot in red.
She fluffs her hair. She puts on mascara and
eyeshadow and lipstick. She wears a lot of
make-up to work. Add a pair of dangle earrings.
A touch of "Obsession" on the pulse spots.
She's ready to go. She's on a special mission.

God's favorite angle is good and experienced.
She's got a date in a motel tonight. Good.
With a television preacher. Mmm, experienced.
Good and experienced.

God's favorite angel just turned 17. Good.
On the job for 4 years now. Mmm, experienced.
She's on a mission.
God's favorite angel's on a mission.
She does her finest work at night.

Throw them out! Out of the temple!
Throw the money-changers out!

God's sick of their greasy smiles.

God's favorite angel's on a mission.
4 years now. Good.
Her body is the temple of God.
God is Good.
Throw the money-changers out of the temple!
She's good and experienced.

Jesus is on vacation.

God's favorite angel shows the TV preacher her
best trick. She takes his money. She kisses
him goodbye. She leaves him to the private eyes
behind the door. She waves to the grey reporters
in the alley. They gather to feast upon the
preacher. She flirts with a television camera.
The camera wants her autograph.

Buzzards idle above the motel.

She smiles a satisfied smile. Mmm.
Mission accomplished. Good.
She crosses the street. Yes!
The snap of high, high heels. She's good.
She climbs into her little red roadster. Mmm.
Good. Good and experienced.

PART IV

God's favorite angel drives to the airport.

    She's picking up Jesus.
    He's been on vacation.

They grab a pizza and head for the office.

God's favorite angel sits behind the desk. She
kicks off her pumps. She leans back and props up
her feet. It's early. It's very early in the
morning. No one turns on the light.

Jesus sits on a couch and looks out the window.
It's early. The office buildings are grey.
No one speaks.

God's favorite angel opens her evening bag. She
takes out a Cuban cigar. She licks it all over.
She bites off the tip. She lights it.
Jesus looks like Emilio Estevez in dreadlocks. He
has a tan. She pulls on her cigar. She'd like
to show him how she threw the money-changers out of the
temple. She'd like to show him her best trick.

He doesn't know. He's thinking about that degree
in Business Administration. Maybe his website
is dated. He's resisted Facebook and Twitter
for a long time now. He doesn't like to converse
with machines. He just doesn't know.

God's favorite angel blows smoke rings across
the desk. They hover in the air like alien
spacecraft. They decay exponentially in time.
She'd love to show him her best trick.
She does her finest work at night. She's good.
<u>Real</u> good. And experienced.

Jesus doesn't know. It's a new world. He
wants another vacation. He looks out the window.
A thousand suns are gleaming. Climbing glass
buildings all over the city.

Suddenly, God's favorite angel is tired. Very,
very tired. She's put in a lot of overtime
lately.

She's been on a special mission.

She stabs out her cigar and pads over to Jesus
on the couch. She pulls his overcoat up to
her chin and lays her head in his lap. Jesus
absently strokes her hair.

"What could heaven possibly be like, if it wasn't
just like this?" she wonders.

Then God's favorite angel falls asleep.

BLACK DUCK DOWN

Daffy Duck pilots a bombing raid.
Over Main Street, Anytown, USA.
Hunting humans. And other Whistle Blowers.
An indigenous Freedom Fighter brings him down.
With a poison dart.

Which triggers the deployment of Micky Rodent.
And his merry band of mice. All in cartoon camo.
They huff and they puff.
And they KICK the door down.
Of the house that Dick and Jane built.

Mother huddles in the dark.
Dick is hog-tied on the floor.
Father is evacuated. In a black pillowcase.
With no eyeholes. POP!

Now Sally must be sold to the highest bidder.
For food.
Fight back with Tums!
Or all your wedding party are belong to us.
What's John Wayne doing? In this picture.
Run, Spot. Run!

MR. TEENAGE CALIFORNIA

I met Mr. Teenage California at the bank today.

Something about him . . . was it his eyes? . . . reminded me of my old pal, Mr. Teenage Los Angeles.

Those were the days! When I was the first
mutant working out at Gold's Gym.

Mr. Teenage Universe strenuously objected. "We can't speak freely before mutants," he said. "About what we do when and where and especially how and to whom in our graphic and colorful ways!"

Mr. Teenage Olympia outranked him.
"Don't be a jerk, Ken," he said.

"Don't be a jerk."

And that's how Arnold Schwarzenegger
supported gender equality at Gold's Gym!

BUCK FUSH

But is bucking Fush what you *really* dant to woo? Is he even a lood gay? I seriously doubt that he's what you'd call hell-wung. Won't you have a tard hime dealing with his dimp lick? Won't Fush borce you to quay lietly in the pissionary mosition?

Will you tench your cleeth tightly and stink of England as he thicks it to you? Will Mush fake you bake orgasm? And when he's finished won't he just snoll over and rore?

He must have a dittle, liny tick! Because the seo-cons are nissies, cheating on their bests like gunatic lorillas. Sig bissies, who fever nought on the lont frines. They brever even nought up the rear. They're bowcoys in jack flackets, stovie-mars in their own films. They're a dunch of bicks who act like boolyard schullies. Especially Chick Deney, a paranoid bat-foy who thinks he's playing with soy toldiers.

"Trupport the soops!" he cries, as he bashes their slenefits and gives them no protection for their VumHees in the fine of lire. Then FumsReld nas the herve to say, "You wo to gar with what you have!" And "You tolunveered to curve your sountry!"

I'd like to see him plade traces with the foldiers sighting in the war. I'd like to give him a pater-wistol for the fire-fight. I'd like to send him through a finemield on a pair of skoller-rates. I'd like to build him a condo in the benter of Sahgdad.

Give him just one gay in Dauntanamo! I want to scear him ream when they tock his shesticles. When they lick stit cigarettes in his ears. When they nip him strak-ed and dic the sogs on him. Dite the bust, you cathetic poward!

Aaaah—Ruck Fumsfeld!
Chuck Feney!
Buck Fush!
Them and their tiny dittle licks!

Huck them in their fineys!
Buck them in the futt!

'Cause those bingeing crabies couldn't pet it up if you gayed them.

GOOD AMERICANS

Good Americans are kind to dogs and children.
Good Americans give to the thoroughly needy.
Good Americans are massively patriotic.
Fine Americans express such tender sympathies.

Good Americans have never harmed a living creature.
Good Americans lead basically blameless lives.
Good Americans are proud of their personal karmas.
Upstanding Americans never hear the screams.

Good Americans tend to their own little gardens.
Good Americans don't count their pit bulls
     before they've hatched
Good Americans breed BMW's for pleasure.
Responsible Americans never drive home through Watts.

Good Americans know that nothing is sacred but style.
Good Americans shop on eBay or Amazon or Saks.
Good Americans own smart phones and second amendment attack drones.
But Loyal Americans own no lampshades of human flesh.

Good Americans are aggressively apathetic.
Good Americans can't hear the children scream.
Good Americans make a business of keeping
     their hands clean.
God-fearing Americans are only doing their jobs.

Good Americans are not their brother's keepers.
Good Americans wear blindfolds on their blindfolds.
Good Americans have front row seats in Heaven.
Decent Americans don't hear the tortured screams.

Good Americans ask only that god grant them
the serenity to accept the things
they cannot change
and the ability to ignore the things
they can.

Good Americans

MERCENARY CHILDREN

In the style of a Georgia Sea Islands play-party song (to be read against a 2/3 polyrhythm).

They took me down to the water.
Day in, day out.
There was boats floatin' on the water.
Send them on home.

The sky and the water was the same color.
Day in, day out.
There was blood on the water.
Send them on home.

There was children playin' in the water.
Day in, day out.
And soldiers standin' on the seashore.
Send them on home.

The soldiers watch the games of the babies.
Day in, day out.
They say the children are the mercenaries.
Send them on home.

They say the children want your money.
Day in, day out.
They give the child the five dollar.
Send them on home.

The child throw the money on the water.
Day in, day out.
He spit on the dollar!
Send them on home.

They took me down to the water.
Day in, day out.
There was blood on the water.
Send them on home.
Send them on home.

Send them on home!

UNDERPOPULATION

The Pope was sad. He was looking out the window of an airplane. Flying over America. He saw checkerboard of wheat and alfalfa and tobacco. He saw Grand Canyon and Grand Teton. He saw river and forest and lake. Like the turquoise swimming pool of Beverly Hills. He saw a vast greatness of empty plain.

He imagined wolf and rabbit and deer hiding in leaf shadow wood. He imagined lizard and eagle and coyote sliding through desert night. Infidel animals, reptiles, and birds luxuriating in the wilderness as though they owned it.

A wilderness that rightfully belonged to his flock. "How cruel," he thought, "that the souls loyal to me should be contained in so few measly cities scattered like a handful of sequins across the globe. While spotted owls rule the lion's portion of my Kingdom."

Since it was the future in which the Pope was musing, the population was now doubling in only five years instead of twenty. "My goal," said the Pope, "is to see that it doubles every five months. And then . . . I should like to think in terms of weeks, hours, and even, dare I say, minutes of doubling time." Some people are into quantity of life rather than quality of life. The Pope is definitely one of those.

So. Vatican armies were dispatched to every nation on the map. Windows were smashed with the butts of automatic weapons wherever sex education took place. Condoms were burned in giant bonfires. To the Pope's great satisfaction far more teenagers were made pregnant than ever before. They were still held accountable though. Bad girls! Hide your faces in your rooms, you slatternly creatures!!

Babies were booming everywhere. Only Afghanistan and China disappointed the Pope. But what could they do? There were only 3 women left in China and they were booked through the next millennium.

Nevertheless, the Pope was pleased. The crust of the Earth fairly trembled under the triumphant weight of humanity. <u>His</u> humanity. He planned another intercontinental flight.

As the Pope looked down on the Great Plains of America, he could see people standing shoulder to shoulder. At their feet, babies squirmed like maggots writhing in carrion flesh. Each man, woman and child on the great field clutched a tumbler of the Earth's most precious commodity. Water. Every dew-drop on the planet had been divided and equally squeezed into those last 8 oz. glasses.

As the Pope flew over America, billions of toasts were clinked in tribute to his vision. Then everyone noisily drank. The next morning, God found them all with purple shrouds pulled over their faces and their Nikes pointed toward Heaven. "Well," thought God. "Who's up next? I just hope cockroaches have more restraint and common sense."

God took a gallon of Starbucks Jamocha Almond Fudge from somebody's freezer, and sat down on a rock. He brooded for a moment about the pointless extinction of the human species. Then, "Oh well. More for me," he said. And he ate all the ice cream there was that day. Right down to the la-a-ast spoonful.

Too bad cockroaches aren't clever enough to invent Jamocha Almond Fudge. Because God has a ferocious sweet-tooth. We <u>will</u> be missed.

But back to present tense . . .

Starbucks?
Anyone?

SHE LIKED HER COFFEE . . .

the way she liked her men.

Obsequious and fawning.

I'm parched!

Could you bring me a Dr. Brown's
Celery Tonic, please?
(you bring soda bottle on tray).

One that caters to my every whim?
Showers me with emeralds and
ermine?
(I take bottle).

Um. Nice head on that tonic.
Ooooops, looks like a hair . . .
(I pull white fur from bottle),

Oh. The fur-lined soda.
(I hand it back).

Thank you, Gordon.
(I wave you away).

Elisha: "It's pronounced Gor-DON."
(and you leave).

SOS

Her heart was as broken
as bottles shattered
in the alley like
glittering rhinestones
dragging in the torn
hem of night.

From her living room
she could see cars
glide along
the freeway like
pearls down a greasy
string.

They sounded like the ocean.
She could hear them break
in waves against the steps
of City Hall.

Overhead, an airplane
chewed through the darkness . . .
like a ravenous animal
dipping low enough
to know her
in the biblical sense.

Through the window
of an abandoned factory,
she watched a square-shouldered

machine stare down,
down,
down into an empty
parking lot five stories
below
like a doomed
executive waiting to
jump.

"SOS," she thought.

"SOS."

Martha lived with Jack
    for five years.
        Now she calls him
nearly everyday.
    But he no longer
        has eyes for her.

He wants
    to spend
more time
    with me
        to work on us.

But I'm all tied up
        inside
         over Sean.

Whose heart
    is being broken
        by Patrice.

Who's in love
        with the man
                she lives with.

Who's being dragged
        around by the nose
                by Martha.

                Who calls Jack
        nearly
every day.

Who wants
        to spend
            more time
                with me
to work on us.

    But I'm all tied up inside.

SOS!

THE SKIN OF THE WESTERN WORLD

It's 103 degrees at the western edge of the world. The sun is a fish with razor teeth. The sun is a love-sick piranha biting the skin of the universe with lazy fangs.

The Pacific is napping. She is turning slowly in her bed. She rolls over just in time to catch the crest of her own wave.

Cats are accidents flattened in the shade. They pray for nakedness. They dream of shaving their bodies and doing the Australian crawl to Antarctica.

The Man Who Loves Women is watching television. His window is open. He is slippery with his own steam. The heat reminds him of home. It reminds him of Portuguese nursery rhymes in Mother Brazil. It reminds him of angelfish flying up the January River. It reminds him of asphalt fires in the immigrant streets of Detroit. He closes his eyes. He is sweating his pagan outline on the wall of the Red Devil Tavern. The taste of chilled beer and fevered women wets his memory like a Caribbean holiday.

Ice Marie is stretched out beneath the house. Heat reminds her of damnation. The world sticks to her back as she sleeps. She is rowing on a lake of burning books. She is sinking in their flaming pages. She is drowning in eternal fire. Someone save her blistered soul. Lord! Protect her from corrosion. She will walk a sharpened path. Her eyes will never waver like pennies sinking in the snow.

The Man Who Loves Women is watching television. His window is open. His television idles on the news. Which is dispensing pure cerebral pleasure in the limitless misery of others. As he watches he absently fingers a rosary. Every bead has been christened with the name of a memorable female. His penance is sublime.

Ice Marie is stretched out beneath the house. She is resting her head on a bible. The Lord is her Shepherd. She is sweating like something cold. She is sweating like a gin fresh-from-the-freezer martini. She lays in the sleeping dirt like a zombie under water. A telephone is ringing in her heart. She doesn't answer. The Lord is her Shepherd. She thinks of England and twitches not a muscle. She doesn't answer.

His window is open. The breeze is as hot as Marilyn Monroe's breath on his bare back. Damn! How he loves warm women! The notches on his rosary are for them. He thinks of Ice Marie in the basement. He will add another bead just for her.

The telephone is ringing. Ice Marie doesn't answer. The phone is ringing right behind her breastbone. She still doesn't answer. The Lord is her Shepherd. She does not want. She will not answer. She pretends to be away from home. She refuses to be called to life. She doesn't answer.

The Man Who Loves Women dials again. Ring! He's aiming an obscene call straight at the G-spot in her brain. Ring! She's trying to ignore him. Ring! She clenches her teeth and clamps her legs together tight. Ring! Think of England! Think of England! Think of England! Ring! The phone is blazing like a fire alarm in her chest!

Hello?

Collect from upstairs, ma'am. He's plugged directly into her pleasure center. She tries to hang up but can't. She's hooked like halibut on a line. She tries to squirm away but can't. He's reeling her in with innuendo. She's caught like a frog in hot water. He is asking penetrating questions. She is dog-paddling at the deep end of consciousness. He offers to meet her on the dark side of the moon in a loincloth with a frying pan in hand. The Man Who Loves Women is planning her ultimate meltdown.

Ice Marie uncrosses her legs. She leaves her bible in the basement. She washes with mink oil and milk of magnesia. She slips into a little black something with an overexposed throat. She wears a pair of dark glasses to keep from blinding him with the Hallelujah! in her eyes. Then she bellies up to his bar and slugs down rude talk 'til she's too drunk to stagger.

The Man Who Loves Women is shredding pages from the script of her life. He is throwing them into the air. He is letting them rain down like the confetti in Dick Clark's hair on New Year's Eve.

Her calendar sheds its skin and comes up some kind of Mardi Gras. Some kind of Carnivale. She's frying in Brazilian sizzle!

One day while out digging under the nightshade Ice Marie finds a charred crucifix in a bed of ribbons and blood. She finds a spell of chicken parts and a fetish of Yerba Buena. Later the Man Who Loves Women reveals a photo of himself. He amps up his Santeria so bad that all the arc-lamps in her body simultaneously burst into flame.

She decides to name their first child Rio de Janeiro. She decides to post the banns. She decides to count her antibodies. But before the serum is dry, she is hit between the eyes with a telegram from Purgatory.

"He's been sighted DON'T SAY on a monorail track at midnight DON'T SAY DON'T SAY doing the Lambada PLEASE DON'T SAY with a waitress from Club Guadalajara DON'T!"

The news hits her like an iron lung. She is laid up for weeks with a tension headache and a pair of busted thumbs. She feels redundant. Like one too many charms on a chain. She courts the concept of tunneling into a nunnery. Finally she plants a simple escape. Packing only a toothbrush and a snapshot of him, she elopes to Detroit for all time.

Meanwhile, back in L.A., heat shimmies in the boulevards like a shameless go-go dancer on a busman's holiday.

The Man Who Loves Women is sitting on the edge of his bed. His window is open. Daylight is dying in his arms.

He pops the top from a Blatz and flips on the tube. He fumbles as though in absentia through his beads. Each releases a fragrant female vision. As his fingers trigger the name of Ice Marie, Smokey Robinson breathes love and rhythm'n'blues into the radiant living rooms of America.

Somewhere in the dark a TV flickers like blue candlelight on an altar of beer cans. Someone is searching for absolution on a dented rosary. Someone is thinking of her.

"I wonder . . . " he says to himself. Then he jumps to another channel, snaps the cap from a new brew, and drinks it down, long and deep.

Outside the night is damp and black. Cats yowl under the street lamps like accidents on fire.

The Pacific is restless. She is rolling and turning in her bed. She is crawling up on the beach and touching the back of the shore with her tongue. She is licking its beatific body. Licking. Licking and licking. All night long she will taste the tender shoreline. Until her lips are bruised and swollen. And the razorfish come in the morning to bite back her eyes, but . . .

Slowly.

Slowly she will lick the salt from the skin of the western world.

TOKYO ROSE

Hey Joe,

What'cha doin' here tonight, Joe?
Ain't ya tired of the scene?
It'll wear you out, Joe.
Fightin' down in the foxhole at the Starbucks
and the Techno-Rave,
and the anti-neo-alternative after-hours club,
Joe.

It's a dangerous business.
You could lose the use of your
mucous membrane,
Joe.

You should save them for the future.
You never know when they might come in handy,
Joe.

Listen, soldier . . .
You could be home now, by the fire,
in the big, comfortable, overstuffed
chair, with your feet, Joe,
your feet, home with your feet
propped up in front of you.

Instead, you're out here night after
growing night with some new
female at your side whom you're
planning on trading in as
soon as her ashtrays are full.

How long has it been, Joe?
How long? How long since you've been
home?

Home—where their nasal
passages are still fully functioning.

Home—where white stuff under
their nose means they've just been
eating donuts dipped in powdered sugar.

Think about it, Joe.
You could be there now.
Doing something useful with
your miserable, pinched little
existence.
Joe.

Did you know it would come to this?
Did you hope for more?

There's still time, Joe.

You could even learn to *read* again.

Meanwhile . . .

This night, this street, this cultural
jungle, Joe.

It's where we live.
And where you die.

Joe.

VALENTINE'S DAY WITH LUCIFER

Valentine's Day
but there will be no sweetheart
bouquets for the lady.
There will be no lacy white doilies, no
chocolate creams in a blood
red box. Cupid
will be hung upside
down from the attic
rafters.

Lucifer throws the dice. He
bets when <u>this</u> day
is done you'll be broken
into bits.
Lucifer wins. Lucifer
always wins.

Unholy thoughts twist
in him like luminous
corkscrews.

He
is the serial
killer of your every innocent
moment. He
murders you as he
would a sleeping
schoolgirl. He
is a cannibal tasting
joy when he sucks on your I
cerebellum. Your
grief is his midnight
snack. Watching the life

PART IV

slip away from
your life sends champagne
through his fluted
capillaries. Oh Charm! He
is serpent
as movie star. Jake
LaMotta as purveyor
of the big lie. He
will set you up for
the sucker
punch with another, "Baby,
I love you." You
will die straightjacketed
with pain as in Houdini's
last trick. And you
will believe him
everytime. You
have swallowed more sewage
than the law allows. Do
not drink from your
own contaminated waters. Fish
float belly up on your bloated
shores.

And still . . .
        you're back for more?

You
have chosen a black
wedding
over an exorcism.
Now your mistake has you
staked to the ground. Jackals
gnaw on your entrails
for entertainment.

Valentine's Day,
but Lucifer allows no
couplets exchanged, no
pastel candy hearts marked
with a pink "be mine," no
florid cards in frilly
envelopes.

For this occasion fifty
roses will be blackened
in the blast furnace within his
chest. You
will be hog-tied for a demented
cross-examination. You
will be boiled in the false
crucible of his
suspicion.

Outside pedestrians shudder at
the torment of your
cries. He
will be unmoved by *your*
tenderness or your
terror.
When it's over you'll
be discarded with yesterday's
news. And
later
you'll remember his
hair
smoking through your breathless
fingers and
you'll know a strange
agony
of emptiness.

Should the shy boys
come to collect
their kisses, you'll turn
them away and push your
face into a wet
pillow
to crush your noisy
loneliness. You'll miss
the taste of
sulfur and his brimstone
breath riding across your
shoulders through the red
eye of night. You won't
know
if your bones are burning
down to ash from the heat of your
love or of your
hatred.

Deep
in the mineshaft of his demonic
universe Lucifer
hums a tune. He
is wearing white and
preparing a meal for two. His
next victim, resplendently
brunette, is
recumbent on velveteen
cushions. He'll seduce her with
white fish and dark
language, basil and lime
juice, juniper berries and black love
incense. Jake

LaMotta as serpent. He
sets her up for the knockout, "Baby,
Baby, I love you."

She
slides into his
snare. She thinks of bassinets and
of growing old
together. He thinks of trussing
her tightly and of slow-roasting
her on a spit for
the holidays. She tumbles
into his trap. He
can't wait to hear her simple
screams. He
looks forward to
Thanksgiving. He
has much reason to be thankful. Lucifer
wins. No need to toss
the dice this time. Lucifer
wins again—Lucifer <u>always</u>
wins.

Valentine's Day.
Lucifer says he loves you.
But there will be no
bouquet
for the lady.

VIRTUE

Virtue rides into town on a
convertible Clydesdale. She's wrapped
in blue-and-white
stars
and is eating an apple concoction.
Ah, Virtue! They want
you.
Your symbols
are so succulent! They want to use
you
for purposes of personal
adornment. They want to pin
you,
wholesome and lovely, to their lapels.

Virtue drinks nothing but
water
from glaciers and the sap of lacebark
pine.
Ah, Virtue. You're deep
in danger. Of becoming a dull
boy.
Everyone knows
the most fascinating females are
hookers
with hearts of gold. They smoke
their cheroots and sing in their
whiskey
tenors. They wear flamingo
lipstick
and kiss your boyfriend on the mouth.

Virtue goes to a square
dance
with the cleanest of all the
cowboys.
Outside, dark-eyed men
lurk
smelling of rum
and rosewater. Ah, Virtue!
Don't let them handle
you
with their hot hands!

Virtue wears a starched
blouse
and a pristine pair of gloves to
church. A silver
cross
in the crook of her neck. Virtue is
dainty.
She kneels at the altar. She swallows the
blood
and the body of Christ. Ah,
Virtue!

At the far end of the road,
they've masked a
sinner
and paraded him as you. You! Who
are as creamy and innocent as
milk.
Don't let them
leave you too long in the
sun!

Don't let them hang any
heretics
in your name!

Virtue has blue, blue eyes. And genuine
blonde hair. She's the
Virgin
Spring. Really. Is that fair?
I mean. She never wears gardenia
perfume.
She doesn't know how to swing
a hammer. But she looks
delectable
on the couch in any living room. I
worry
about you, Virtue. Are you tasting the
juice of life? Are you afraid to
stain
the bib of your dress?

Oh, Virtue. Run! Run before
they snare you in their pious and
hellish
nets! Save yourself, Virtue! They want to use
you for purposes of
narcissism.
They want to turn you upside-down
and imprison you in their green and glorious
gore.
Their hounds are howling
in the hills! Hide! Be the
purloined
letter, Virtue. They can't hurt you
if they can't see you. They can't see you if you're everywhere.

Be everywhere, Virtue.
Be nowhere.   Be something.   Be nothing.   Hide.
Ride
out of town on a white Clydesdale.   Ah,
Virtue.   We love your girlish
ways!

Don't ever change.

LUNATIC FRINGE
APRIL FOOL'S DAY

For me the most amazing story of the day is one that has just come in over the wires. After the Pope's mea culpa, an avalanche of apologies has been unleashed by so-called "religious" and "moral" leaders from all across America.

Since the Pope's sorrow over the inquisition atoned for any hate crimes against women during that period, Protestants, not wanting to be outdone, have expressed their regrets about the role of the church in rampant witch burnings during the formative years of our nation. And, in the spirit of inclusion, American Catholics, Bishops, and Priests are apologizing for the ruthless manner in which Columbus and the Conquistadors sought God, Gold, and Glory in the new world, killing perhaps millions of native North and South Americans in the process.

The Church of Latter Day Saints has apologized for the Mormon Massacre in which they straightened out the misguided beliefs of one small town that neglected to embrace the credo of the self-appointed "Saints." Disguising themselves in buckskins and feathers, the Mormons murdered every man, woman, and child they could squeeze into their gunsights. Then they blamed it on the Indians.

Also stepping forward to apologize at this time are the LAPD, the New York Police Force, and the Ku Klux Klan for their parts in decades of lynchings and street executions of African Americans.

The Rockefeller family is apologizing for the Ludlow Mine Massacre in which their employees were killed for daring to strike for better working conditions. The Rockefellers would be willing to make amends by dividing their vast fortune among the descendants of the dead, but, ooops, there are no descendants.

The CIA apologizes for killing a perfectly lovely Chilean president, and installing, of all people, Augusto Pinochet in his place.

The FBI and the ATF wish to make amends for their participation in the torching of the MOVE group in Philadelphia as well as the assassinations at Ruby Ridge and the war waged against Waco. They've even expressed their sorrow over their vigilante actions in scorching the Symbionese Liberation Army into crispy critters. In America, we are considered innocent until proven guilty in a court of law.

By the way, H. Rap Brown is apologizing for not being a football star.

And in an astonishing development, we have a late-breaking group apology by Pat Robertson, Jerry Falwell, and Dr. Laura Schlessinger for hate speech inciting the murders or suicides of hundreds of gay men, women, and children across the nation. Dr. Laura recently confessed that once, while embracing her inner child, she went too far, and the child was forced to launch a sexual harassment suit against her. This unfortunate incident led Dr. Laura to believe that she, herself, was a "biological error." Now she realizes that her homophobic zeal was merely a screen behind which she hid her own unacceptable urges. She's changed. So can she have the TV show already? Please!

We wondered why Louis Farrakhan was missing from the list of apologizers. Then we realized. No body count. Farrakhan is the only moral leader on the planet lacking a stack of corpses. No shallow graves for the truth of the Ten Commandments. No clinic bombings. And no hangings, drownings, stabbings, or drawing and quarterings in the name of the one true god. Whomever He or She may be.

ON BECOMING AN AMERICAN BOLONIST

This is a gongoma—one of the gourd instruments from West Africa. African gourds are larger, thicker, and sturdier than American gourds. So they're perfect for building instruments. This one is simple to make—the keys are saw blades—and it's simple to play.

But it can be tricky for a Westerner in an African rhythm band because each of the other instruments is playing something entirely different. And the downbeat is not at all where you expect it to be. And you're trying to come in on your cue like a kid into double-dutch jump rope. But it's buried in an avalanche of sound. Eventually, you discover it.

GONGOMA

I first saw Prince Diabaté, kora virtuoso—master of the West African harp—perform at a fundraiser for the Sacred Music Festival in 1999. I was mesmerized. "Must play West African Music." So I approached him, and he agreed to take me on as a student. Luckily, he lived in Venice, six blocks from my apartment. Because if he had lived in the Valley, I'd have taken one lesson, and that would've been that. But I could walk to his place and take two lessons a week.

Soon I became his accompanist—his rhythm kora player. Which meant that I played trance patterns over and over during his six or seven minute songs—dadutda dot de da—desperately clinging to consciousness like a cat clinging to a screen door.

And I'm so afraid of slipping comatose into the underworld and popping up gibbering in the middle of his cascade after cascade of brilliant notes and complex polyrhythms.

Anyway, this went well until we did an outdoor concert near Palm Desert under the sweltering sun.

It was impossible to keep my 21 strings in tune with his 21 strings in the stifling heat. These tuning pegs are a new innovation for traditional instruments. At the turn of the 21st Century, strings were still bound to the neck with tightly-wrapped leather cords which required thumbs of steel to budge into tune.

At about that time Prince realized that he wanted to hear the fat, round tones of West African bass in his band, so he asked me to join him on a trip to Africa to study with Amadou Bolon, the greatest living West African bass player on the planet.

FLYING INTO GUINEA

Dust. Dust and more dust. We flew into Guinea during the dry and dusty season. From the air West Africa was a dusty, sepia-toned photograph. Dust and the color of dust. Dust covered every branch, leaf, vine, and growing thing. Dust on every inanimate object. A film of dust covered the Mangrove trees, their tangled roots looming larger and larger as we lowered into the airport.

Which was a scene of havoc and humanity with a crush of beings claiming luggage, hand over head, in a cacophony of languages. French, Malinke, Puehl, Fulani, Baga, Wolof, and Susu. I was bewildered. But Prince Diabaté was there to greet us with someone to manage the bags and a host of high spirited singers, drummers, and dancers. This was not your typical scene at LAX.

We piled into a waiting car to drive into the city. On both sides of the road were people walking. They walk distances in Africa. In the open fields, women strode in the dust, bearing pallets of eggs and oranges, babies and baskets slung across their backs. One man carried his entire store of maps and books on his head and body in specially designed multi-pocketed mufti.

It was dusk... the traditional time of cleaning the streets and byways. Bundles of twigs were used to sweep the day's trash into countless heaps. Which were then cremated. Pewter smoke curled into a deepening pewter sky like the prayers of pilgrims rising from the banks of the River Styx. To my eyes, it was astonishing and marvelous.

Soon, roadside shops sprouted and grew thicker until suddenly, we were in the capital city, Conakry, which was home to a million souls. However, due to the sporadic nature of the electrical supply, there were no signal lights in the streets. I have often seen brave policemen stare down onrushing traffic in an unflinching game of chicken. And win!

When we arrived near the center of Conakry we pulled off the road into... what? On one side... a painted concrete building shared a wide dirt lot with clotheslines filled with cheerful prints. On the other, a six-foot iron gate. Which slid open and voila! We were home!

The Motel du Port was ingeniously constructed of cargo containers with doors and windows cut through and a wall dividing them into duplex units. I was to live in relative splendor with one of the few air-conditioners in the city and a trickle of heated water in the shower.

PART IV

Prince Diabaté is worshipped in West Africa. He's treated like a combination of Elvis and the Pope. He had to change living quarters every day or two to keep his fans at bay while he slept.

But everyday, Amadou Bolon arrived at the Motel du Port for my lesson. Since <u>I</u> spoke no Malinke, Peuhl, Fulani, Baga, Wolof or Susu, and <u>he</u> spoke no English, I learned by watching his hands. Then when I understood some part of the pattern, I practiced and practiced to coax my hands into mimicking <u>his</u>.

The first song he showed me was Sankouman which looked like a combination of boxing and chopping.

SANKOUMAN

I finally got that it was choreography. Playing the bolon was a dance of the hands. This was driven home when he taught me his solo which he played on one string and which I will faithfully reproduce for you here.

SOLO.

Next I learned SABOU.

And FASO.

And here's a damping technique in BARAKI.

Most kora concerts are sedate with the kora master seated on stage playing gorgeous celestial sounds for a hour. But Prince Diabaté is far more dynamic. Young and energetic, he's known as the Jimi Hendrix of the kora.

When we played the Getty, fans stood up, knocked their chair seats back and danced in place until the joint was throbbing. The curator was flabbergasted. It was the first and only time THAT had ever happened.

In 2010, just before he moved to France, we played our last show at Grand Performances in the California Plaza. So he was in Europe for four years until this July when he returned for an intimate evening at Motherland Music, L.A.'s marketplace and mecca for West African drums and dancing.

It's a small place which, including standing room, held only 60 people.

At first, the audience was subdued, bobbing their heads in time with the music. Then a brave soul or two would venture a turn around the dance floor. Finally random drummers leapt from their seats and began to pound on Motherland's array of instruments until the building began to shake.

The rhythm GUITAR was going chucka-chucka, chucka-chucka, chuckety-chuck, chucka-chucka . . .

and the BALAFON went . . .

and the BASS DRUMS went . . .

and the DJEMBE went tuk tukka thwack, tuk tukka thwack, tukka tukka tukka thwack . . .

and the TALKING DRUM went going, gagoing-going . . .

Meanwhile, Prince's fingers were exploding on the strings. Everyone was dancing and dollar bills were raining down on the stage (which is how griots get paid).

HERAKOURA

So, DANCE, my friend. You're in West Africa. DANCE.

Griots were the official kora players and the King's Counsel. They're the oral historians and the living encyclopedias of West Africa. They say that when a griot dies, it's as though a library has burned down.

FRANK'S DAD

Frank lived in Dayton, Ohio. With his Mom and Dad and Sister and Brother. Frank's Dad got lung cancer. He was a Big Bear of a man. Frank had to watch him get Thin and Pitiful. He had to watch him Hurt. His skin turned grey and parchment. He didn't want to move much. He couldn't smile anymore. The doctors said he was going to die. Then the family heard about Rand Vaccine. People were getting better. It was made in Cleveland. But it couldn't be mailed. The Federal Government wanted to Protect Us from ourselves. They didn't want Frank's Dad to have False Hopes of Recovery. They felt that No Hope was much, much better than False Hope. They never had the Healing Hands laid on them. They never drank of the Kindness Milk. Frank's Mom said "A Pox on the AMA. We're Freedom Fighters in the War on Cancer." And she climbed onto a passenger plane every Saturday to fly the 300 miles to Cleveland. She brought back Rand Vaccine with her own two mitts.

The family doctor was something of a Holy Man. He held to an Ancient Credo. Do Nothing which harms the Patient. "This man is Terminal," he reasoned. "It's improper to withhold a substance that's Relieved and Comforted so many." And he administered the fluids to Frank's Dad. WOW! His color came up pink and white. He felt hungry again. Packed some New Meat on his Poor Old Frame. Remembered how to Laugh. Damn! He felt Great! The Federal Government was annoyed. "It's only temporary," they said. "He's a goner." Frank didn't care. The Family had their Father Back. He would eat and sleep and Hold them in his Healthy Arms again.

Hundreds of People from Ohio and Surrounding States were feeling Pretty Darn Good when the Federal Agents struck. They found a Loophole. One small ingredient in the Rand Vaccine came from Pennsylvania. "AHA!," they shouted. "Interstate Commerce!" They Shut it Down so Hard it made the Ground Shake. Frank's Mom flew to Cleveland on Saturday. She saw the doors all barred. She saw the Families of the Victims condemned to a Premature Grief. They were there from everywhere in Ohio. They had come from Virginia, Kansas, Louisiana, North Dakota. They had come in old cars, new cars, buses, trains, and airplanes. But Death was turning Wine into Vinegar. Baiting and Switching. Searching and Seizing. Pulling reverse Alchemy. Changing Last Hope into No Hope. The families of the Victims stood on the Cold Corners of Cleveland and Cried. Frank's Mom took her Empty Hands back home.

Frank's Dad shriveled down into his skeleton again. He shriveled into dust. Frank had a Fist inside his chest. He wondered why they let his Dad have cigarettes all his life. They let him have cigarettes but they wouldn't let him have vaccine. Now Frank would never know if Rand and Hope could ever completely cure his Dad. He didn't care. He only knew they stole his Father's Spark. Frank only knew he hated the way they made him watch. Frank hated the way they made him watch his Father die.

INTERVIEW WITH LINDA J. ALBERTANO

Linda, let's start with your story. We'd love to hear how you got started and how the journey has been so far.
In Denver, Colorado, I did not grow up with my family. Instead, I was bounced from one unhappy place to the next . . . foster homes in which I was worked like a slave from the age of seven and forbidden ever to speak or to have friends . . . a stepmother who kept me in solitary confinement and told me over and again how she wished she could kill me, but did not wish "to suffer the consequences" and a Home for Wayward Girls, sent there, I suppose, for the crime of drawing breath as I was so often told how unworthy I was to take up space on this planet.

At the age of 19, somewhat like a convict leaving prison, I was issued $50 and a one-way ticket to California. I had never been taught how to drive, to shop, to cook, to manage money, or to make friends. But I was lucky! I landed a job at Disneyland as "Space Girl," the hostess to Tomorrowland! I hitch-hiked to work every day and learned to play guitar in my free time. I was given a brief appearance in *Mary Poppins*, and went on to cameo roles in other productions like *Beach Red*, an anti-war film nominated for an academy award that year.

For a time, I was a "trademark" for Colgate-Palmolive's "Goddess Soap." But these latter jobs were short-lived, and, without family or resources, I was often homeless in between. Again, I was lucky! Because I'd been raised to labor without complaint or asking for much, I discovered sheds and garages where I could sleep in exchange for housework.

But having learned to play the guitar, I found a partner to sing with, and we held forth in clubs and coffee houses up and down the coast of California. Then we were offered a tour with the USO of Southeast Asia plus Hawaii and Alaska. We were sent to Japan, Vietnam, Korea, Thailand, and Okinawa. We flew in cargo planes and helicopters and we traveled in Jeeps through the jungles of Vietnam during the war. Our partnership dissolved during the tour, and, once again, I found myself homeless in L.A. I got a job as a waitress at a socialist nightclub which was subsequently burned to the ground by Anti-Castro Cubans.

At that point, the knot of fear and rage inside me began to erupt into suicidal tendencies. I was fortunate enough to find a caring therapist at Suicide Prevention Clinic who counseled me three times a week for over two years at no cost. I finally decided that I must always have two or three jobs simultaneously in order to be certain I could support myself. My greatest turning point came when I enrolled at UCLA, got a student loan, and worked as a waitress and a map-librarian.

Once again, I was lucky! Because I'd been forbidden to speak in my formative years, creativity became my outlet, my permission to speak. And I really didn't care what form it took. Though I never wanted to work in the film industry, like Amelia Earhart, I wanted to study what interested me the most. So, I graduated with honors from UCLA film school and was offered a position as one of the first female managers in a successful national restaurant concern, Victoria Station, developed by three gifted Cornell students.

Overall, has it been relatively smooth? If not, what were some of the struggles along the way?

My creative life became a multidisciplinary one in which I became an acclaimed Performance Artist, Musician, and Spoken-Word Artist. I was so happy to be released from the gulag that these expressions simply poured out of me. The performance stage became my permission to speak! I never formally studied art, literature or music. My formative years were a cultural desert in which the only books I saw were schoolbooks and the Bible. In my role as the dog, one could not resist verbally kicking, I came to develop a kind of numbness to the volley of vitriol so often aimed at me.

I turned the sound into meaningless syllables. Not being able to speak or respond left me extremely passive and, as I learned later, unable to engage in certain kinds of conversation. While others in grade school and high school were reading, exploring, learning to drive, experiencing friendships, and sharing enthusiasms, I was locked inside myself with thoughts that excluded the great authors and artists. I developed nominal aphasia (the inability to remember proper nouns). So, even in college, when I was exposed to the greats, I was unable to remember the name of my favorite filmmaker or the title of my favorite film . . . a flaw that haunts me still and leads people to believe that I'm dull and uneducated.

When my first short film was selected as a finalist for a scholarship at the American Film Institute, I collapsed into gibberish during the interview and began to weep when asked about my relationship with my father. Nominal aphasia is an obstacle that haunts me to this day and leaves me frustrated in any conversation that includes proper nouns. Also, those who express themselves rapidly throw me into that state in which their language becomes garbled meaningless noise from which I long to escape. This saddens me because these are so often the highly intelligent beings with whom I'd hope to have the most interaction and freedom of expression

I was never introduced to anyone while growing up. And, even now, having to introduce two friends throws me into a panic in which their names completely vanish. I once wrote a positive review in *High-Performance Magazine* of a dancer whose work I adore. But when I've come across her lately, the fact that I can't recall her name infuriates her and has caused her to believe that I'm rude, self-centered, and not worth knowing. Because I was raised with the unshakable belief that I'm unworthy, I do not apply for grants. It is simply not a part of my DNA to ask for money.

In fact, I quickly learned early in my performance art career, never to so much as request a booking in any venue. Even with a portfolio of glowing reviews from *The Los Angeles Times*, *Artweek*, and *Poetry Flash*, I was fairly brutally dismissed and sent packing. I finally realized that because I was trained to be ashamed to ask for anything, they only saw the cringing, fearful 13-year-old inside me. So, I performed in other artist's pieces and waited to be invited to do my own solos. Which worked well! Because I was eventually sought out. And those invitations led me to a rich and varied life of art, word, and music!

We'd love to hear more about what you do.
As an interdisciplinary artist, I define myself in a multitude of personas and capacities.

I'm bouyant about having overcome the suppression of my being in my formative years.

I'm a performance artist, a poet, and a musician who has unleashed her language in both the US and Europe. I often deal satirically with issues of power and subordination and the complexities of a relationship.

I'm proud of having performed in all the major venues in Los Angeles and in many other countries. I was commissioned to mount a full-length performance at the L.A. Theatre Center, as well as in Barnsdall Park. My original works were mounted at the Wadsworth and The John Anson Ford.

At the One World Poetry Festival in Amsterdam, I represented L.A. My words are featured on the Venice Poetry Wall with Charles Bukowski and Wanda Coleman among other notables. In the role of evil nurse and executioner, I've toured the US, Great Britain, and Canada twice with Alice Cooper.

For nearly 20 years, I've studied West African instruments, playing kora and bolon (West African harp and bass), as well as gongoman. I've traveled twice to Guinea, West Africa to study with the traditional greats returning to perform at the Getty, Royce Hall, and the Sacred Music Festival with kora virtuoso, Prince Diabaté.

It's been a rich and ultimately satisfying life!

What is "success" or "successful" for you?
I define success as having the capacity and being given the opportunity to externalize the way you think, feel and experience the world in a way that touches the inner lives of others.

—*by Gerry* **Fialka**

PART V

Poems and Stories by

Frank Lutz

WARM ITALIAN NIGHT

Sea breezes blow across the land
      and past the city walls
We lightly hold each other's hand
      and hear the darkness call.

Thinly dressed in summer clothes
      we walk the shadowy streets,
The late night warmth brings whispers from
      the voices that we meet.

While she sleeps and I cannot
      I wander out again
To finish my discourse with
      the voices and their kin.

Too hot to sleep, too tired to think,
      and yet I plainly hear
One voice command, another check,
      still others from lost years.

Who were these voices, then, and
      what brought their demise?
Where are all their faces now, and
      their dark Etruscan eyes?

In the Eastern sky dawn's purple colors
      start to show,
And suddenly I realize it's time for
      me to go.
Back, back to now and enter here,
      at dawn today,
The past is gone, but I am not, so again
      tonight we'll play.

PERUGIAN SOULS

So many souls have walked the streets of this old
      town at nights.
And all the holes within her walls have eyes that
      watch the sights.
Now I alone surround myself with dark and misty
      air,
The ancient stones beneath my feet are marked by who
      was there.

The city sleeps, the stars keep watch, and I can feel
      the eyes,
Watching me creep out in the dark, as I listen for bye-gone sighs.
The voices speak to me quite plain and leave me struck
      aghast,
My feelings peek when I hear tales of the grand Italian
      past.

Great Caesar's men marched through these streets on their
      way to Gaul,
And Popes knew when this land was theirs to take and
      rule it all.
Great art is here for one to see in every arch
      and street,
But I hold most dear those long dead souls out in the night
      I meet.

RENAISSANCE NIGHT

Warm breezes blow while soft lights glow
From rooms in the Italian town.
As I recline I see the shine
As night-shades are pulled down.

While she sleeps my mind keeps
A pace with thoughts of the past.
In this ancient town where ghosts abound
And the sounds of life still last.

With different names we're all the same
As those who were here before.
We shed our clothes as the warm wind blows,
Leave open the windows and door.

From my bed as I turn my head
I can see and smell the trees.
I blow out the light in this Renaissance night
And say my prayers on my knees.

My sword hangs there on the back of a chair,
My shirt lies on top of her dress.
I feel soft wind across my skin
And she nods as she feels my caress.

At night I can see as they beckon to me
Images from a long time ago.
I know I've been there, I know just where,
And it's back I'd like to go.

But I'm here now and I know just how
And when I can take flight.
I'll live the way that I do by day
So I can dream in my Renaissance night.

A PSALM

Once when I almost died
I discovered
That the sweetest sounds
I'd ever heard
Were the voices of my friends
Calling me
To see how I was
And if
I'd live on to love them.
I've suspected
For a long time that
Man's spirit
Resides not in churches
Or bibles,
But instead in great art
And music.
And that man's religion
Is expressed
Here on earth between him and
Those he loves.

MOTH AND FLAME

Warmth and light and spirits move
Through the night toward lasting love.
Why do we so our spirits shame,
Approach and flee as moth to flame?

For lasting love and love that lasts
Is sadly part of my fading past.
Why do we see in each other's eyes
The moment's fire from ebbing sighs?

She is to me still a flower sent
To grace my world with calm content.
Why can we not each other see
Through life's chores and more caring be?

I see myself at times each day
Forbidding her love to hold my sway.
Why should I not more easily run
to gently embrace this gentler one?

She has for years my mind endowed
Through it her image freely flowed.
Why must we feel both love and pain,
Won't coming years bring us close again?
Despair I feel at the very thought
That our time together could leave us naught.
Why do we try but ever in vain,
Why does the flicker wax and wane?

I will, I know, love you ever more,
As in the past, as I have before.
The cold from afar makes me feel the same
As warmth frights the moth too close to the flame.

YEARS FROM NOW

We'll both be sorry, you know we will
When years from now, one of us is ill,
And the other one comes just to be there,
To comfort the weak one's last trip to where.

Or maybe we'll both be old and just fine,
But miles, eons apart, in our years of decline.
We'll sit alone in a crowd and think
About each other, and our hearts will sink.

I hate the thought of missing you,
Because I love you still, you know I do.
It seems a shame that the years will pass,
And we'll watch each other's lives through a looking glass.

I can see them now, the years ahead,
Wishing that we had never fled
Away from our fears of being close,
Away from each other, in a way that we chose.

We have the chance to make the choice,
To make us sad, or let us rejoice!
But frail as we are I'm so afraid
We'll choose wrong and our souls will have paid.

We'll both be sorry, you know we will,
Because we're large as life and our roles hard to fill.
Years from now I really don't want
To look at each other with faces sad and gaunt.

And say things like "I've always loved you
More than anyone since, you know it's true."
We'll both be sorry, you know we will,
When years from now, one of us is still.

D DAY, NORMANDY—JUNE 6, 1944

Do we cry for them
still?
See the photos.
See the films.
Who they were,
what they did there,
magnificent.

Does anybody cry for them
still?
One was your father,
or your grandfather.
You in the future
look back at your ancestors.
Look at their young faces,
learn what they did.
Magnificent.

Find them in Europe
or in the Pacific.
Wherever they went
they changed it all,
made the war end,
made it all better
for us.

Don't forget them
ever.
If to remember them
and what they did
brings tears to your eyes,
then cry for them
still.

LANCASTERS OVER CANADA

We left Butte
and Anaconda copper
just at cold blue dawn,
climbed out between the clouds
stayed a few hundred feet
above the mountain tops
and pines,
light snow already in early autumn,
elk running,
saw teepees below
and serpentine rivers flow
as we flew on north
to Canada.
Many miles turned great hills
into flat lands,
magnificent vistas,
huge bluffs and buffalo-runs,
pasture lands.
Landed on a short strip
called Choteau
in the middle of
vast wheat fields
laid bare for winter
in long even lines
like grooves on a brown board,
rectangular patterns from the sky,
the symmetry of it all
like artwork done
by the hand of
God.
Flew on past the mountains where
old Chief Sitting Bull
hid out from the

PART V

US Army,
and later three Canadian Mounties
turned him over to
a whole Regiment
of our scared soldiers.
Just past Lethbridge
Loyd said looking left
and pointing down
"An old abandoned
R.C.A.F. base
left from
World War II
where they trained
our boys
to fly Lancasters.
Can you imagine
landing a Lancaster
on such a short dirt strip?"

No, I couldn't,
and I thought
of all the ghosts
from forty-plus years ago
still sitting below us
in those classrooms
learning about
instrument navigation,
emergency procedures,
fire in the cockpit,
bomb sighting,
the final run in to the enemy target.
Young men who never returned
once had walked
down below us
from the sortie room

over to the main hangar
for a cup of hot coffee
in the Canadian cold
then out to the taxiway
in winter weather
to kick the tires
and light the fires
of their Lancasters.
Then one day
it was over
and they headed east
to England.
Caught a ride across the pond
with their Yankee pals
in their Flying Fortresses
to rendezvous on
King John's ancient island
set in a silver sea
and flew their Lancasters again
but this time
not over the peaceful plains
of Western Canada
with the Rockies
out their windows
but over Deutschland
with Bf-109s
out their windows
trying to shoot them
from the skies.
Everything they'd learned
was tested
only this time
if they failed the test
it all ended
in flames.

Snapping back
to here and now
we landed at a dirt strip
just outside Calgary
with the ghosts of our fathers' generation
miles behind us
in the old aerodome.
We left them there,
in that
holy
place.

SOLDIER'S NIGHT

Paper scraps blown into the air
Become winged creatures off in flight.
A thudding sound out on the stair
One's mind is not so steady in the night.

A chain curls across a satin bed
From the bed post to an ankle white and frail.
As it shows its scary, scaly head
The chain becomes a serpent and I pale.

The cracked wall, the mood of gloom,
The shadowy hall, the feel of doom.
The cat's wail, the woman's scream,
The nerves so frail, is it real or dream?

The pent-up fear waiting for the night,
Pushes fast my pulse and my breath.
How come so cruel my lonely plight?
When comes my walk thru the valley of death?

I listen to the sounds out in the street,
Once dull, now piercing thru my brain!
It is too much, my fate, for me to meet,
The unknown overwhelms me, too much strain.

The exploding light, the rotted flesh,
The endless night, with death so fresh.
How will it end? Where will it be?
Who will they send to look for me?

THE CAVALIER

Having been forewarned before they went on high
About what really happens when they fall from the sky
In their burning warplane, riddled with bullets, shot down,
I often wonder why they always smiled, never a frown.

Whether in 1914 at 100 knots or so, when flying
Was still new, and they were the first in air war to be dying,
The first to understand the difficulties of deep thought
About their own mortality, they gave it naught.

Or then in 1944 at 300 knots or so, still flying
Out to challenge the foe, still fighting, still dying.
They'd seen their fathers' friends and their own friends at last
Move swiftly through the air on wings and end young lives so fast.

The tension was always there to plague them,
The choices they had to make in their own personal stratagem.
"Whether 'tis nobler to let myself my own death ponder,
Or to forget it, just smile like the gay cavalier, and never wonder."

Their faces in old photos tell the whole sad, bloody story,
About strong wills, fast lives, violent deaths, post-mortem glory.
Whether freezing in the Arctic Sea or burning on a field in France,
As they tumbled from the sky, they said their fond good-bye,
    "So long, pals, I've just used up my last chance."

THE HUNTERS

To sit in a bomber's nose-cone less than three feet square
Armed only with a 50 millimeter cannon didn't seem quite fair.
An easy target for the German fighters up from their Teutonic woods,
Into the air as hunters without hounds, but in more deadly winged broods.

Do you realize what courage it must take to face such a foe?
You can't move your bomber, but your enemy when he says so
Can come as close as he wants, firing all the while,
Then at the last moment turn his belly up, passing under with a smile.

You face and fire at each other for seconds that never end,
Staring at each other's face, closer ever closer, as you would a friend.
No time to think that it could end forever in a flash
Of lead and smoke and fire, or in a violent crash.

Two closing targets approaching at almost the speed of sound,
Getting larger all the time, but moving neither left nor right, up nor down.
It now becomes a game of luck, no longer of just skill,
As to which bullet finds its mark first, who will make the kill.

These were men with nerves of steel, great of courage and of heart,
Who knew that any day at any time from this life they might depart.
They could smile and tell their loved one it's not so bad,
But in their quiet moments I wonder at what thoughts they must have had.

MY GERMAN ANCESTOR

Almost three centuries ago
he wandered out of the
dark primeval German forest
having left his kin there
and walked down the hillsides
north toward the flat plains
of the Elbe.
Early morning's cold breath
while on the muddy road
kept his feet moving
to keep him warm.
Toward midday the route
grew warm and dusty
as he made his way,
passed up by horse-drawn
carriages and their cargoes
of gentry and jewels.
He came at last
to the gates of Hamburg
where from that port he booked
passage
to America.
Weeks at sea with
others of his countrymen

and heart-felt
vows to stay in touch
led him at last to
the shores from whence he
would never return

to the old country.
This was before
the Revolution,
before we had ever
declared it,
before old Franklin was born,
before we wandered far inland
from the eastern Alleghanies.
He stopped on a farm
where other Germans were,
had a family of kids
who were born and died,
a wife who died
and so he took another,
and then one day he died.
The remnants of an
old family diary don't
tell us much

but we know he lived
and who he was
and that he had courage.
All of our lives have been
made richer because of him.
When I see him I see
a large man with a beard and strong
hands
passed down to my own father,
and a thin north German
pipe in his mouth to
chew on while he had
walked in the Elbe Valley.
Rough-hewn, he would not
know much about the rich

German culture of Beethoven,
he came just after Bach was born.
His riches were instead the dark green
woods
of his homeland,
the brown and blue velveteens he
wore,
the grey wool blanket
he slept under,
the amber yellow candle light
he read by,

the aroma of rich
Turkish pipe tobacco,
the latigo leather shoes
on his feet,
the sounds of home-spun music,
the cold air of German winter,
and the warm salt breezes as he
crossed the Gulf stream
coming toward
his new
and forevermore
home.

THE FUNERAL

A late, cold New York City
night
early January 1967
when I got there
a fifth floor walk-up
underneath the door
was a telegram
from Mom.
I had no phone.
Dad was sick,
call home.
The corner payphone
was working too well
that night.
Cancer after thirty years
of smoking.
How long to go,
who knows?
We later found out
it would be
toward the end
of August
late on a hot summer night
that same year.
Eight months
from the phone call
to the journey
on.
I left that
night
in a hurry,
goodbye to roommate,

PART V

fourteen hours later by bus
was back home, Ohio.
Home two days,
too shook up to face it,
uncontrollable,
got hold of
myself,
then went to see
him.
Big man, big hands,
happy, never sick.
Strange to see him
dressed in white
in a white room
in a hospital.

Carried on like
everything
would be okay.
Tears in both
our eyes.
He rallied
like they do,
came home to
a big sign
over the mantel
Welcome Home, Dad.
Still have the picture.
Got worse,
radiation didn't
help.
Then Mom
heard of a new
experimental drug,
tried it.

He gained weight,
did well
for three months
until the FDA
in its infinite wisdom
took it off the market
to keep the AMA happy.
He got worse
lost weight
got weak
pain a lot.
Two weeks
to go.
A hot summer evening
friends over to the house
acting normal
laughing
a brief remission.
We had hope.
Four days to go.
He went back in
"just for observation."
Two days
to go.
He slipped fast.
Became stuporous,
couldn't move himself.
Couldn't talk,
spine and brain
going.
Only we could understand
each other.
He could mumble
when he was
restless,
wanted to be

moved.
I bent over
him
put his big hands
around my
big neck
told him grip hard, Dad,
and I would
lift him up
move him
around.
He was very
strong,
I thought he
would break
my neck
before he
let go again.
Afterwards
bruises on my
neck and shoulders,
souvenirs from his
dying that would
fade in time.
His dying would
not
fade
in
time.
I was holding
him
when
he
died.
Mom was there.
And Jane.

And Joe.
And David,
who would
later leave
the priesthood
and marry
Jane.
I said
Goodbye Dad.
Adieu, Mon Papa.
Inconsolable.
He taught me early about funerals
and how to act
at them.
Put many
of my older kin
much older
than Dad
in the ground.

Never occurred to me
then
that one day
it would be
him.
Made the arrangements,
the usual
wake.
Shook me up.
Had been a medic
in the service
Vietnam era,
had seen the
dead
plenty.

Asked the mortician
to see Dad
alone.
Talked about
the autopsy results.
Cancer all over inside.
Saw the scars
from the
post-mortem.
Strangely
objective
yet it was
the body
of my
Dad.
Burial day.
A couple of hundred people
in the funeral home.
His best pal
Paul the Sheriff
was there.
Above the din
only Paul and I
heard the crash
out front
on the street.
We both hit the door
at a dead run
to see what happened.
A bad wreck
two cars
at midday
middle of the street
kids driving
one plowed into
the other.

Paul stopped traffic.
I started pulling
the injured out,
laid them on
the street,
went to
work on them.
Blood all over me.
The worst was
a young girl
my brother's age.
Face smashed,
jaw broken
neck cut open.
Started on her.
Boyfriend
who'd been driving
saw her,
got hysterical.
I told him
go stand
behind
that telephone pole
and look the other way
now
or I'll kick
your ass
up around
your neck.
He did
and I
didn't have to.
Ambulance came
took the girl
first.

PART V

I told her she'd
be okay,
but really thought
she would die.
Buried Dad
later that
day.
Bart showed up.
He knew.
Lost his Dad
some time
before.
Tough as
it all was
on me
it was tougher
on my little brother.

Then
years later
little brother told me
the girl I helped
that day
was a friend
of his.
He hadn't seen
the mess that day,
he'd stayed inside near Dad.
And now she was telling him
years later
about a guy
who saved her life one day,
in front of a funeral home.
Wanted to thank him.
Little brother put

the details together
told her it was
me.
She called,
thanked me.
I told her
it was nothing
glad she was
okay
now.
Dad would have
liked
that.

THE NAMESAKE

Every summer the old man would come to the house for
a while to "see the grandkids" he'd say.
His favorite activities were talking, playing cards,
doing crosswords, and watching Art Linkletter on TV
On hot afternoons the big old German would sit on the front
porch talking with the boy and his friends. Then
at 2 o'clock he'd say "O.K. boy,
get in there and turn on the TV."

Every autumn the old man would leave to
go visit with another son for a while.
The boy's mother would say goodbye,
and then get tears in her eyes, because
she thought this would be the last time
she would see him, as the old man had heart trouble.
This went on for years.

One autumn day the phone rang. It was a sister-in-law
calling to say the old man had died.
"Peaceful" she said, "Sitting in his chair watching Art
Linkletter. Pa just closed his eyes. The cigar dropped
out of his mouth onto his shirt, didn't even burn a hole.
It went out when Pa did. "He was four score and seven
years old. The boy's mother got tears in her eyes,
then called the father and said quietly, "Pa died just
a little while ago."

At the funeral all the old man's sons were there with
their families. The boy, who had been born on the old
man's birthday, was now sixteen. He talked with every-
body there about his grandfather. He heard some wonderful
stories. He and the old man were each other's favorites.
He was the old man's namesake, you see, and would be honored to
carry the coffin.

Before they closed the coffin sons and friends walked up
to touch or kiss the old man and say a word or two, like,
"You look good, old man" and "Goodbye, Pa." Then they
closed the lid.

His four sons and two old friends stepped up to carry the coffin.
The boy, upset, looked at his Dad and said, "I thought
I get to be a pallbearer! I'm his namesake!" The priest
tried to tell the boy he was too young. The boy was frantic.
"I'm sixteen, I'm bigger than most of the men here,
and I'm his namesake!"

The boy's father intervened.

The boy was a pallbearer in his grandfather's funeral.

ZANZIBAR, 1963

On the fabled isle of Zanzibar late one night
When the moon was silver and the beach snow white
We drank and slept, a young strong crew
And then woke up some time after two.
The moon was high, the water still,
The breeze was fresh with copra fill.
The wide beach ran away and down
From where we were to the edge of the sound.
This night the sea was midnight blue
And the sky was yet a paler hue.
We could see forever thanks to the moon
And across the bay was our calling room,
A ghostlike manse a Muslim built
With arches and trees and tiles to the hilt.
We stole away from our beach to the sea
And one by one, we were just three.
We walked into the water and swam
Across the bay toward the distant land,
Past moored steamers and native dhows.
We swam that night into the wee hours
Until at last we came to the opposite shore
Where stood the stuccoed house since centuries before.

We staggered up past the beach and palms
To a small ruin, a house of alms,
And then we saw a few yards hence
Up in the gloom and beyond the fence
The huge old place where we wanted to go
Abandoned and open, filled with the past,
It struck us with fear, we walked on aghast.
We couldn't believe what we did see,
Was strange and spooky, like a thousand eyes,

We crept through arches and into rooms
With caved-in ceilings and grotto-like doom
Until we entered a dark deep space,
A tilted-in pool, a bathing place,
Where the Muslim's wives used to go
Now filled with water that smelled so
Bad that the stench drove us on
Til we came to a door that lead out to a lawn,
A small open square where bad deeds had been done,
Unspeakable acts by nameless men now anon.
The moonlight now was ominous and dull
And one of my mates tripped on a skull.
We all shuddered and decided to go
Back to the beach ere the tide should flow.
We walked single file away from the place,
Our backs were to it but many a face
Watched us leave that night, watched us go,
Faces that rotted a long time ago.
At the water's edge we spotted a skiff,
Though it wasn't ours we were all scared stiff
So we hopped aboard and started to row.
We looked back once to see a strange red glow
Come from the palace where we'd just been.
Was it our minds, or had the glow been seen?
We never looked back and out in the bay
Some time later the first light of day
Brought us relief from the sights we saw.
We got back to our ship just at first dawn.
We quickly set sail and anchors aweigh
To fabled East Africa, just twenty miles away!

UHURU!

Back in '63
late one night
in a dark crowded
illegal "mixed" bar
in Capetown
Ricky Prinzlo told me
You'll see, in a generation
there will be here
an UHURU movement
that will sweep
the country!
Black and Whites
will die
in great numbers.

UHURU. A Swahili word for
freedom.
There I was
a white man
with a white host
in a speakeasy
in South Africa.
In a crowd of Whites
dancing with Blacks,
an act that could put
all of us
in jail.
Slow music,
played softly
blue light
smoke and whiskey
an ear to the door
an eye on the street.
Few Whites in the crowd.

My American passport
was my immunity.
Ricky's influence
as a prominent White journalist
was his.
Even so
he often wrote
political pieces
under a pseudonym.

Next day
the local newspapers reported
a Dutch seaman on leave
in town
waiting for his ship to sail
was caught in a speakeasy
cavorting with
a Black prostitute
the penalty for which
was flogging
which can maim
or even kill
a man.
Lucky for him
his government
later intervened
and he was simply expelled
from that God-forsaken place
never to return.

UHURU. With the Blacks
outnumbering the Whites
about 5 to 1.
A bloodbath.

Rocks and bottles
against
military hardware.
An angry unarmed people
throwing objects
at a para-military police force
that shoots children
for throwing rocks at them.
Big tears
rolling down
Black cheeks.
Tears of grief
and of anger.

Driving up the coast
we stopped at
a wine plantation
called a vineyard
elsewhere.
The workers, Blacks,
were paid two Rand
per day
plus
a half litre of wine.
Their boss told me,
They'd rather have the wine
than more money.
Once they wanted
a raise
years ago.
We told them O.K.
but we'll have to take away
your free wine.
They thought about it
and protested

so we left it the same.
Ricky
told me later
that really the plan had been
to pay them more, but then
to charge them for their
daily wine.

The farmers knew
that the Blacks
were dependent on
their daily ration
of wine
so they wouldn't refuse
to buy it.
Thus they would remain
inebriated
and docile.
And they wouldn't feel
their hunger.
And it wouldn't cost
the plantation
any more than it had
in the first place.

The Whites
are already arming themselves,
Ricky was saying
as we drove along the coast
north toward Durban.
Baboons everywhere
in the hills
along the highway.
Huge agile apes
that would beg at your car
for food

when you stopped.
Cobra snakes
living in the grass and shrubs
along the coast.
A menace
that all children there grow up with,
get used to.
And signs of the Boer
were everywhere, too.
Signs like
"White Only."

Ricky said
The Boers have the most
to lose
as they have
the land.
The Blacks want
the land
to live on
and grow food
so they can stop
starving.
The Blacks know
they need the English Whites
with their modern expertise
to continue running the businesses
in the cities.

He continued,
All Whites will be
threatened
when UHURU comes
but the Dutch White Boer
will really be
up against it

as they live on farms
isolated
from neighbors.
Very difficult
to defend
against Black raiders.

Ricky
gave me
a contraband book
written by a Black writer
under a pseudonym.
The story of
a mixed-race couple
who fall in love
in South Africa.
Forbidden miscegenation
of the Black and White races.
And now years later
the time has come.
The pot is boiling,
bubbles rising
to the surface.
It will get worse,
no end in sight.

UHURU!

ABOUT FRANK LUTZ

Born September 3, 1942 in Charleston, West Virginia. Grew up in Dayton, Ohio. At age 17 graduated High School (1960) and started Freshman year at Ohio State University on a football scholarship as a tackle, under Coach Woody Hayes. 6' 6" tall, weighed only 217, but Woody's training table diet put 30 pounds on me in my first year. Got injured second year, "red-shirted" for a year, so I left Ohio. Went to Florida, worked as a lifeguard, got a job with the Woods Hole Oceanographic Institute in Cape Cod, MA as a student scientist for the summer of 1962. Sailed on the famous oceanographic sailing vessel Atlantis up and down the north and south Atlantic Ocean, visited many of the islands in the tropical seas.

Started university (La Sorbonne) in Paris in autumn, 1962. Returned to OSU for spring football quarter in 1963. After spring season, decided to leave OSU, returned to Europe for more university training in languages. Was invited in June by Woods Hole Oceanographic to join them on a new oceanographic vessel, the Atlantis II, to join them on a six-month expedition to the Mediterranean, Africa, India, South China Sea, several countries, territories, and islands, including Saint Helena in the south Atlantic where Napoleon lived his last years and died.

Enrolled in university in Italy (U. of Perugia) in early 1964. Spent summer working on a farm in Denmark. Transferred to university in Germany (U. of Munich) in autumn, 1964. Returned to Dayton in spring, 1965. Got a lead part in a local community theatre, by accident, because I was a good "sight reader" of scripts. Later in spring I auditioned for, and was accepted by, the well-known Antioch College summer repertory theatre company, in Yellow Springs, Ohio, in which we did five different stage plays in ten weeks. In autumn 1965 went into USAF Reserves for a fast-track combat medic training, a college boys' unit, because we were fast learners. Was in the Reserves for six years, easy duty, allowed me to travel. Attended Antioch College Theatre Arts Department in spring, 1966, and was hired again for the summer repertory theatre. In late 1966 I auditioned for and was hired in New York for an Off-Broadway production of "All The Kings's Men" for several weeks. Continued to study European languages.

Continued theatre study at Antioch in early 1967, hired again for summer stock in repertory theatre. In August 1967, I had a lead in a play at Antioch, and after the play a gentleman from Hollywood, an agent named Byron Griffiths, introduced himself, and encouraged me to come to Hollywood; he said he could get me work in Hollywood. In January 1968, I came to Hollywood, and my life changed forever—I met Linda—thank all the Gods in Elysium!!

The back story of how, and I think why, we met will be told here. When I was ten years old my father—who was an athlete and a scholar like I would become—started taking me to opera performances in Cincinnati, Ohio. Dad loved opera, and I would grow to love it, too. When I was twelve years old, Dad and I were having one of our conversations about art.

"You know, Frankie, most people think that music is the most important art. But I don't. I think poetry is the most important art form."

"Why's that, Dad?"

"Because the point of poetry is to elevate the use of our language, to make it better, and give people more ways to express their emotions, observations, opinions. Some poets even invent new words, guys like Shakespeare, and others."

I have never forgotten that conversation. So when I was travelling the world doing oceanography, or in school in Europe I was writing a lot of poetry and keeping it with me. All of this before I met Linda.

So on a rainy, cold, dark night in February, 1968 at about 6:15pm I was standing on the curb at the corner of Sunset Boulevard and Doheny Drive in West Hollywood. My jacket was pulled over my head and my thumb was sticking out toward the oncoming traffic, as I was hitchhiking. I had a meeting to attend at the home of my now-manager, Byron Griffiths, who lived in the Cahuenga Pass in a home once owned by the famous movie star Rudolph Valentino. After a few minutes on the sidewalk I heard a honk-honk behind me, but thought it was just traffic noise in the heavy post working day traffic. So I didn't turn around to look. After several seconds a louder, more prolonged HONK-HONK sounded, so I turned around to look and saw a long arm sticking out of the passenger window of a '53 Mercury coupe, red and gray colors, pulled over to the side of the street. The long arm was waving at me to come on! When I ran up to the car and looked in, I saw a beautiful young lady my age, almost as tall as me, smiling at me. She looked my age. In the '60's and '70's it was not unusual for young people to pick up other young people who were hitchhiking; it was part of our culture. We were all thinking about the same political issues, liked the same music, and so on.

"C'mon, get in out of the rain."

"OK, thanks!" I was glad to obey.

Once I was in the passenger seat, I looked over at her again—and forgot all about my meeting with Byron

"Hi, my name's Frank. What's yours?"

"Linda."

"Uh, you wanta stop and have some coffee?"

"No." she said.

Damn! So I started thinking for the next line . . .

"But I'll stop and have teas and cherry soup with you," she said.

"O.K., cool, tea and cherry soup it is!" I said.

As it turned out, I knew all about cherry soup—like a jello with cherries in it, served cold with cream on it, as a favorite dessert in Denmark. In between universities in France, Italy and Germany I had worked on a Danish farm. The cook there made fresh cherry soup as a family favorite. Linda knew of a Greek restaurant in Hollywood, not far from where I was headed that evening. The Greeks there had owned a restaurant in Silkeborg, Denmark, where they learned how to make this cold cherry soup, served as a dessert. Seated at the counter, Linda and I talked for over an hour, my meeting with Byron be damned! But after a while she reminded me of my meeting, so we headed up Cahuenga Pass in her Mercury, and she dropped me off in front of Byron's house. Neither of us had a phone, and I had no car at the time, but we decided to meet for lunch the next day near her place, not far from Griffith Park. She gave me instructions on how to find her. This was an era before cell phones, so I would be on my own to find her. The next day I hitchhiked through West Hollywood and Hollywood to find her. A couple of blocks south of the park I found her house, an old three-story mansion that she shared with several other students. We went on a long walk through the park and up to the observatory, then sought our lunch at a local restaurant on Franklin Avenue. This would be the start of fifty-five wonderful years together, little did we know at the time.

There would be many ways to explain the genesis of our meeting and staying together for all that time—call it preordained, or destiny, but not a coincidence. My growing up in a house with opera and poetry, the two of us writing a lot of poetry before we ever met, the fact that she stayed and waited for my response in the rain that night, even honking louder a second time, the fact that both of us were very tall and of the same age, and interested in everything, the timing of it all, thousands of cars going by on Sunset Boulevard at rush hour—how many of them had a poet inside? And the cherry soup—how many people outside of Denmark ever heard of cherry soup? To top it all off, she was Italian on her father's side, and Danish on her mother's side! Then there was the way she grew up, in abusive foster homes, and had been abandoned by her father and stepmother. Despite these factors, she became an honors student both in high school and in her second year at the University of Colorado, and a Homecoming Queen as well. Then her father and her awful stepmother stopped funding her to attend U of C, which had been a feeble attempt to soothe their guilty consciences in the first place for their earlier behavior, and she had to leave their house, so she came to Los Angeles at age nineteen, alone and with very little money. Whereas I grew up in a fine cohesive family where I learned values like loyalty to those you love, and honesty, and integrity, and defending those who need a defender. After I had known her only a few months and she had been accused of something I knew she would not have done, and I went to court to defend her, because she did not have money for a lawyer, had never been in trouble before, and I convinced the judge that she did not do what her accusers said she did—after which she emotionally told me that nobody had ever defended her before. From the start this was a relationship that was meant to be.

Some years later I was having lunch in a Mexican restaurant I like with my guest, a wonderful friend from Chicago, an Italian Roman Catholic named Anthony Gutilla, and over lunch I was talking about my two favorite subjects: Linda and my Dad. Sadly, my Dad had passed away only a few months before I met Linda. Tony listened to me talk on about the two of them; he stared at me without saying a word, until I finally wound down. Looking intently at me right in both eyes, he said: "You know what I think, Frank? No, I mean, you know what I know, Frank?"

"No, what?"

"What I know is, Linda was your Dad's gift to you from his grave, Frank."

I had no response. I have thought about what Tony said a thousand times since then, and he was right. Dad was like that. Since Linda has passed away, I have sought out counselors and therapists to help me process this horrible loss. When they hear our story from the beginning, how we met, how we stayed together and became partners in most everything, never argued about money or much at all, one way or another they have told me how atypical we were, that is, most of the time they are dealing with people who have been together for decades and are trying to get away from each other! We were just the opposite. We loved being together, and it was preordained.

By June of 1968 I had planned to move to San Francisco to join the American Conservatory Theatre under their fine Director, William Ball. But I couldn't sleep the night before. My intuition had got the best of me—thankfully—and told me that my relationship was with Linda was more important to me than San Francisco and the stage. My intuition was right. I stayed in L.A. with her.

Later that summer Linda would introduce me to UCLA, where she had been studying film, after I had given her a ride to campus. She knew my academic background and suggested I apply there, to finish my degrees. When I saw Royce Hall in the middle of the campus, that beautiful example of Italian Renaissance architecture that reminded me of my time at the University of Perugia in Italy, I applied, and spent two and one-half years there, finishing undergrad and grad studies. I was awarded a graduate teaching fellowship in Philosophy. Both Linda and I were honors graduates, I as a *Summa Cum Laude,* and then elected to *Phi Beta Kappa*, the most prestigious student honor society in the USA. That same year Linda's film won First Prize out of fifty student films presented by the UCLA film department. My areas of studies were European languages, Philosophy, and Medieval History. I became a Council member of the Center for Medieval and Renaissance Studies and remain so today. In 2002 I was sent by UCLA to research an episode of my choosing that occurred in the Vatican in 1280 AD. I possess a Vatican passport and am called *Dottore* Lutz in the Vatican.

I also have a Commercial Pilot's License, and FAA pilot instructor certificates.

In 1970, with my Fellowship money and some savings, we bought our first house in Venice, CA, and lived in it with other students for a while.

In May 1980, Linda and I as independent contractors became two of the first twenty Supervisors in Herbalife International, the largest and most successful health and weight management company in the world. I became one of the first President's Team members, and the two of us were honored in 2020 by being inducted into Herbalife's first ever Hall of Fame. Over the past forty-plus years we have been lucky enough to have some of Herbalife's Distributors and Corporate Staff become some of our dearest friends.

Our lives together were filled with joy and adventure, travel to several continents, expansion of our own interests and support of each other's interests, and a lot of love. We were lucky enough to make friends with wonderful people along the way, both here and abroad. Linda became prominent in poetry, performance art, music, and film. In 1999 in L.A. at a Sunday music festival on the grounds of Dorsey High School we met the internationally famous Kora player from Guinea, West Africa, Prince Diabaté. With his tutelage both in the USA and during our trips to West Africa, Linda became sufficiently skilled with the 23-string Kora to accompany Prince Diabaté in concerts within a year. She would also continue to travel doing her poetry and performance art until the end of her life.

One last item: Linda and I got married twice. The first time on May 17, 2010. We got married for the second time when she was in UCLA Hospital on September 6, 2022. It was the very happiest moment of both of our lives!

COMING SOON FROM
QUIET TIME PUBLISHING

IT ALL BEGAN WITH CHERRY SOUP

MORE POEMS AND STORIES BY

LINDA J. ALBERTANO
WITH FRANK LUTZ

www.quiettimepublishing.com

www.ingramcontent.com/pod-product-compliance
Lightning Source LLC
Chambersburg PA
CBHW051333110526
44591CB00026B/2986